Doubles Tennis Tactics

Louis Cayer

International Tennis Federation

Human Kinetics

Library of Congress Cataloging-in-Publication Data

Cayer, Louis.
 Doubles tennis tactics / Louis Cayer; International Tennis Federation.
   p. cm.
 ISBN 0-7360-4004-8 (soft cover)
 1. Tennis--Doubles. I. International Tennis Federation. II. Title.
 GV1002.8.C39 2004
 796.342'28--dc22

2003026760

ISBN: 0-7360-4004-8

Acquisitions Editor: Martin Barnard; **Production Editor:** Melinda Graham; **Assistant Editor:** Scott Hawkins; **Copyeditor:** Kathy Knight Calder; **Proofreader:** Erin Cler; **Graphic Designer:** Nancy Rasmus; **Graphic Artists:** Melinda Graham, Tara Welsch; **Photo Manager:** Dan Wendt; **Cover Designer:** Keith Blomberg; **Photographer (cover):** Tom Roberts; **Photographer (interior pages 19, 20, 27, 28, 29, 31, 35, 37, and 209):** Quebec Tennis Federation, **(all other interior photos unless otherwise noted)** Tennis Canada; **Art Manager:** Kareema McLendon; **Illustrator:** Tim Offenstein; **Printer:** United Graphics

Human Kinetics books are available at special discounts for bulk purchase. Special editions or book excerpts can also be created to specification. For details, contact the Special Sales Manager at Human Kinetics.

Printed in the United States of America   10   9   8   7   6   5   4   3   2   1

Human Kinetics
Web site: www.HumanKinetics.com

United States: Human Kinetics
P.O. Box 5076
Champaign, IL 61825-5076
800-747-4457
e-mail: humank@hkusa.com

Canada: Human Kinetics
475 Devonshire Road Unit 100
Windsor, ON N8Y 2L5
800-465-7301 (in Canada only)
e-mail: orders@hkcanada.com

Europe: Human Kinetics
107 Bradford Road
Stanningley
Leeds LS28 6AT, United Kingdom
+44 (0) 113 255 5665
e-mail: hk@hkeurope.com

Australia: Human Kinetics
57A Price Avenue
Lower Mitcham, South Australia 5062
08 8277 1555
e-mail: liaw@hkaustralia.com

New Zealand: Human Kinetics
Division of Sports Distributors NZ Ltd.
P.O. Box 300 226 Albany
North Shore City
Auckland
0064 9 448 1207
e-mail: blairc@hknewz.com

I would like to thank the International Tennis Federation (ITF) for their confidence in my writing of this book. I also thank the dedicated staff of the ITF for their contributions throughout this process. Special thanks to Stella Maslen, who supported me from the start with revising the text, drawing the diagrams, and taking photos. Without Stella, this book would not be the same. I am also grateful for all the players that I had the chance to work with over the years, from the doubles interclub ladies at Nuns' Island Tennis Club in Montreal, to the Canadian Davis Cup players and professional players from whom I have learned a lot. Finally, thanks to Tennis Canada and Tennis Quebec, who provided the use of photos for this book, and whom I've enjoyed working with all these years.

—Louis Cayer

A number of people have worked very hard over the past three years to make this book on advanced doubles a reality. Of course the book could not have been produced without the efforts of Louis Cayer, former Canadian National Coach/Davis Cup captain and coach of the gold-medal-winning men's doubles team at the 2000 Olympics in Sydney. Louis was the main author and led the editing of the book.

Dave Miley, ITF executive director of development, was instrumental in initiating the book and supported the project throughout. Miguel Crespo, ITF research officer, assisted and contributed at each step of the project, while Machar Reid in Valencia, Spain spent countless hours organizing the material before publication. It is also important to acknowledge Victoria Billington and Clare Gale, at the ITF office in London, for the vast amount of work they both put into the preparation of this book.

Our thanks also to the ITF Coaches Commission members, the ITF development officers, and the other ITF development department staff who have assisted and advised in the preparation of this book.

We are sure that players and coaches throughout the world will enjoy *Doubles Tennis Tactics* and find it useful in their efforts to develop an advanced doubles game wherever that might be.

—International Tennis Federation

CONTENTS

PATTERN AND DRILL FINDER

SERVER PATTERNS

RECEIVER PATTERNS

RECEIVER'S PARTNER PATTERNS

RECEIVING TEAM PATTERNS

PREFACE

Whereas singles play may attract the most commercial interest and media coverage at the professional level of tennis, doubles is typically the heart of tennis at the club, recreational, and amateur levels of the game. Doubles is a great team sport for players of all ages and all levels. Furthermore, doubles combines the positioning, movement, and shot selection patterns of one doubles team with that of the opposing team, offering players tactical possibilities over and above those that commonly characterize singles play.

The presence of players at the net when serving and returning reduces most of the rallying that occurs in singles. Therefore doubles becomes ever more exciting, because attacking and counterattacking or defending patterns of play interact with many net play situations.

Because this book is geared toward advanced doubles performance, we have structured the information with the assumption that both the serving and receiving teams want to take the initiative on the point from the outset (i.e., from the first two shots). In order to gain this edge, it is critical to maximize teamwork with respect to proper positioning and movement. If the two partners coordinate their positioning and movement well, they force their opponents to execute increasingly difficult shots (such as a difficult return for the receiver or a difficult first volley for the server).

Finally, even if television coverage often neglects doubles, important advantages accrue from mastering doubles play:

At the professional level,

- it is an Olympic sport and as such commands a great interest in tennis in general in many countries;
- if a player loses in the early singles rounds on the pro tour, participation in doubles can provide additional match play, hospitality, and prize money; and
- during international team events like the Davis Cup and Federation Cup, the doubles match often determines the victorious team.

At the competitive level,

▌ you can compete in many doubles tournaments and leagues—club, interclub, intercity, and interschool—that offer great fun; and

▌ doubles offers a team aspect of tennis for those who prefer team sports to individual sports.

At the recreational level,

▌ it is the perfect game for having fun and finding new friends, since every club offers round-robins, parties, and social events where doubles is predominantly played; and

▌ besides the normal men's, women's, and mixed doubles categories, many fun pairings can be made—such as pro-am, parent-child, age combining over 100 years, and so forth.

For player development,

▌ competing in doubles complements singles play since it provides players, especially juniors, a great opportunity to develop an all-around game. Indeed, because players have only half of the court to cover, they often approach and play at the net with greater confidence. This focus allows for more extensive and specific practicing of serves, all types of volleys, lobs, smashes, and angled passing shots.

If you are involved in tennis, you have played and will surely continue to play doubles. By implementing the different patterns in this book, you will improve your game and be in regular demand as a doubles partner.

Along with this book you may want to order the video, the International Tennis Federation's *Doubles Tennis Tactics*, which is available from Human Kinetics. The video demonstrates how you can improve your doubles game through using patterns outlined in this book. In footage taken during Davis Cup and Federation Cup matches, the patterns are demonstrated by world class tennis teams such as Sébastien Lareau and Daniel Nestor (2000 Olympic gold) and former number one teams like Leander Paes and Mahesh Bhupathi, Paul Haarhuis and Jacco Eltingh, Mark Woodforde and Sandon Stolle, Venus and Serena Williams, Pete Sampras and Alex O'Brien, Tim Henman and Greg Rusedski, and Boris Becker and Michael Stitch.

INTRODUCTION

Great doubles teams have the ability to cover the court effectively with proper positioning, movement, and poaching actions. They also execute shot selections appropriate to various playing situations when serving or receiving.

In *Doubles Tennis Tactics*, the International Tennis Federation (ITF) addresses three important elements for successful doubles: court coverage, shot selection, and teamwork. You will enjoy the practical format of the book because the ITF selected the most frequent patterns of play encountered in playing doubles.

■ **Court coverage.** The real art of doubles resides in effective positioning, movement, and poaching. In this manual you will learn the exact areas you have to cover as the server, server's partner, receiver, and receiver's partner and what areas you must cover as a team. Diagrams that show you where to stand and where to move illustrate these coverage areas. As for poaching, everyone agrees it is important but very few players do it frequently or successfully. Therefore, we have written a special chapter at the beginning of the book (chapter 2) that systematically addresses what you need to know about effective poaching. You will learn the different types of poaches (reaction, anticipation, command or signal, I formation, and Australian formation) that are necessary when serving or receiving.

■ **Shot selection.** Chapters 3, 4, 6, and 7 present each of the four positions you play (server, server's partner, receiver, and receiver's partner) and cover the different shot selections each position requires when you play matches. For example, in chapter 3 you will see that the server's first volley has to be different according to six different receiving team positions or movements after the return. If you train only a general deep crosscourt first volley, you may find yourself stressed when receiving teams come in or poach after the returns. Therefore, not only the techniques but also the tactical decisions have to become automatic when encountering different situations. These skills are best trained through the tactical patterns of this manual.

■ **Teamwork.** Chapters 5 and 8 present specific team patterns for you to discuss and practice with your partner. Chapter 5, for instance, will help you to successfully implement the different types of poaching covered in chapter 2, to become a wall when both of you are at the net, to decide who takes the middle and who covers the lob, and so forth.

▌ **Planning and charting patterns.** Since there are many patterns to train and different types of opponents to play against, we have added chapter 9 for planning and chapter 10 for charting and anticipating opponents' tactical patterns. This material should prove very useful both for coaches and for all competitive players.

To help you to practice these patterns, the book presents drills based on a systematic 3-step model using basket feeds, live feeds, or cooperative play. (You will find the model of this 3-step progression in chapter 3; thereafter, generally only one of the three drill options illusrates a pattern.) **Basket feeds** develop skills with maximal repetition, as the coach controls the feeds and introduces the ball to train the specific skill. Basket feeds could initiate a learning drill having all the players on the same side, or it could set-up a specific playing situation. **Live feeds** use the skill in a more realistic situation as the ball is actually played to the athlete practicing the skill. **Cooperative play** simulates game situations, but to ensure enough repetition of the skills being trained, the players are requested to cooperate by initiating the point in a certain way before playing it out.

All of these drills can be performed by male and female players with or without a coach. Advanced players can do all of the patterns provided in this book simply by doing the cooperative game situations. It is important to note that tactical training requires decision making, therefore most of the drills are structured so that the players will have to choose between at least two options while perfecting their skills.

One final piece of advice for all readers to remember is to choose the best partner available. This recommendation remains as true today as it was in yesteryear, and we hope that by reading and implementing the patterns outlined in this book, you become that very player!

KEY TO DIAGRAMS

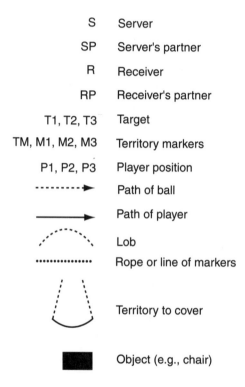

S	Server
SP	Server's partner
R	Receiver
RP	Receiver's partner
T1, T2, T3	Target
TM, M1, M2, M3	Territory markers
P1, P2, P3	Player position

Path of ball

Path of player

Lob

Rope or line of markers

Territory to cover

Object (e.g., chair)

Note: Pattern and drill diagram descriptions assume right-handed players and although the examples are provided on one side of the court only (deuce or ad side), the same logic applies to the other side. Also, most diagrams are conceived for serve-and-volleyers but the drills can be easily adapted for a server who prefers to stay back.

PART I
DOUBLES FOUNDATION

We open this manual on doubles tactics by discussing two important issues that are fundamental to doubles tactical training. These issues are the different game styles in doubles (chapter 1) and the importance of poaching for effective doubles play (chapter 2).

▌ Doubles game styles—Most people think that there is only one way of playing doubles, and they implement tactics that do not necessarily fit their own strengths or styles of play. Therefore in the first chapter we outline different game styles, including their characteristics, strengths, and weaknesses. This material is also important for coaches who want to individualize their objectives or team up their players effectively.

▌ Poaching—Everyone agrees on the importance of poaching, but very few players poach frequently when serving or receiving. Therefore we provide an extensive chapter specifically on poaching. You will learn the differences between poaching per reaction, anticipation, command or signal, the I formation, and the Australian formation. This information can both motivate you to try out at least one type of poaching and help you to perform it successfully.

PLAYING STYLES

Categorizing a team of two players who have differing personalities and playing styles is difficult. When observing teams competing against each other, however, we can distinguish between styles of doubles play and differentiate the playing style of one team from that of another. These classifications can be useful to a team in search of an identity and to a coach who wants to individualize his coaching. They provide clearer direction in terms of training and competing as a team.

We will present five frequent game styles of advanced doubles teams: (1) quick movers and poachers, (2) hard hitters, (3) precision players, (4) all-court players, and (5) combined game style players. We will highlight their general characteristics and outline some of their potential strengths and weaknesses.

Quick Movers and Poachers

Quick moving and poaching teams tend to move a lot when serving and returning. Their constant movement creates uncertainty in their opponents.

Most players view them as good doubles teams, since they implement poaching actions very well.

Many doubles players would like to be able to play this game style but do not feel confident enough at the net. If you want to poach more, start by poaching only against defensive returns, then progress to precision returns. These returns are less intimidating than powerful ones. Once you get confident with your volleys and reflexes at the net, you will be able to poach the power returns as well (see chapter 2 for information on how to poach effectively). Table 1.1 shows some potential strengths and weaknesses of the poaching game style.

Table 1.1	Strengths and Weaknesses of Quick Movers and Poachers	
	Potential strengths	**Potential weaknesses**
SERVER	Moves in quickly and therefore can better handle the returns and put away the floaters.	Often does not serve hard because he likes to move in close to the net.
SERVER'S PARTNER	Has a great presence at the net. Is agile enough to deal with down-the-lines and perform successful poaches. The best partner to have at the net.	Subject to lob because of tendency to play very close to the net. Could poach too soon, resulting in the receiver hitting winners down the line.
SERVING TEAM	Speed and movement.	If one server lacks power on serve, it exposes the team to powerful returns.
RECEIVER	Chips or drives and charges, which forces the server to attempt a better second shot with his first volley or groundstroke when staying back.	When staying back on the return, receiver does not always have great second shots since he relies more on his net game.
RECEIVER'S PARTNER	Moves forward and poaches. Creates pressure on the server's first volley. The best partner to have when you return well.	Sometimes neglects to play both back to improve the defense when necessary.
RECEIVING TEAM	Their overall movement and their ability to outrally the serving team when the four players are at the net.	Could be overpowered by big serves and have difficulty returning them.

▮ Fast movers and poachers are always ready to intercept a crosscourt shot in their role as either the server's or receiver's partner.

Hard Hitters

Hard-hitting teams typically seek to overpower their opponents through forceful strokes. They rely mostly on groundstrokes. Both partners are frequently at the baseline on the returns, with the server staying back (especially at the women's professional level) to initiate the point with powerful groundstrokes. This tactic of staying back, especially after the serve, is more the combined result of the opponent's powerful returns and the server's lack of practice doing serve-and-volley.

More and more teams now rely on powerful serves, returns, and groundstrokes to win their points. One of the main reasons is that juniors are brought up with powerful baseline games and often do not develop effective net games anymore. In 2003, there were only seven Association of Tennis Professionals (ATP) men players and two Women's Tennis Association (WTA) women players in the top 100 who were labeled as serve-and-volleyers in singles.

Coaches can take two possible approaches to improving this situation. The first one is to individualize their coaching and not compel all players to serve and volley especially when coaching women's teams. The second approach is to provide more net game drills for the juniors to help them develop an all-around game and provide the option to serve and volley on the first serve, even if they choose to stay back on the second serve. Table 1.2 shows strengths and weaknesses of hard hitters.

Table 1.2	Strengths and Weaknesses of Hard Hitters	
	Potential strengths	**Potential weaknesses**
SERVER	Often uses big serves or (in the case of those who stay back on their serves) powerful ground-strokes to initiate the rally.	When the serve is very hard, the server sometimes doesn't move in quickly enough. When the server doesn't come to the net, she risks having a difficult second shot against the receiver's partner moving in.
SERVER'S PARTNER	Normally protects his down-the-line area fairly well, since he doesn't seek to poach.	Because he relies on his groundstrokes and is not often a natural volleyer, he doesn't put a lot of pressure on the receiver through poaching or I formation.
SERVING TEAM	The power of their shots is often sufficient to hold serve.	Team often lacks shot variations and diverse movements and therefore can be in trouble if the receiver returns well.
RECEIVER	Powerful returns, especially against second serves.	Some backcourt specialists playing with western grips return first serves from farther back, giving net players more opportunity to poach.
RECEIVER'S PARTNER	Often plays both back to improve counterattack with solid groundstrokes.	Not moving forward on the return removes pressure on the first volley of the server, who can simply block the ball back deep crosscourt or to the middle when playing both back.
RECEIVING TEAM	Is mostly effective on slower surfaces when there is time to set up groundstrokes.	Struggles on fast surfaces against good net players.

▌ When both players are playing back on the returns, hard hitters will look to defeat the net players with their groundstrokes.

Precision Players

Precision teams play with great touch and finesse. They move their opponents around with angles, dinks, and lobs, trying to take advantage of any weakness. Fewer precision teams make it to the pro tour, since the hard hitters often overpower them and the poachers move so well that they throw them off balance. This game style is much more common at the senior level, where many players tend to use backhand slices and precision teams focus on exploiting the opponent's game. Successful precision players have the ability to make their opponents look bad; they do not perform flashy shots but hit very accurately and provoke many mistakes. They are normally hard to read because they disguise their shots well. Table 1.3 shows some potential strengths and weaknesses of the precision game style.

∎ Precision players can produce angles that will pull one player off the court, leaving only one player to deal with the second shot.

Table 1.3	Strengths and Weaknesses of Precision Players	
	Potential strengths	**Potential weaknesses**
SERVER	Places and mixes up the serves well. Has good touch with her first volley and is able to execute many variations.	Lacks power and often has a weak second serve that opponents can attack.
SERVER'S PARTNER	Has great hands and can make drop and angled volleys.	Has in general a more laid-back attitude and is less aggressive at the net.
SERVING TEAM	Relies on the consistency of their first volley and good touch at the net to win the points.	Is generally less intimidating as a team; gives the opponents a sense that they can be broken.
RECEIVER	Very deceptive with angles, lobs, dinks, and so forth. Forces the opponents to react.	Opponents are not afraid to poach against her returns. If this receiver doesn't lob at times, the server will sprint in to handle returns.
RECEIVER'S PARTNER	Good hands allow great defense and the ability to place the volley well when intercepting the server's first volley.	Overall, is more calm than aggressive and often doesn't move forward enough to put pressure on the server.
RECEIVING TEAM	Has the ability to mix up shots and keep the opponents guessing between angles; lobs on both returns and second shots.	Serving teams are getting more powerful and agile, which makes this game style less effective at the pro level, but a threat at social and senior levels.

All-Court Players

All-court players make the best teams, since they can implement most of the tactics mentioned previously. They can drive, place, and move well, both at the baseline and at the net. They can adapt to either the opponents or the surfaces. Unfortunately, as there are so many players specialized at forcing baseliners, it is rare to group two all-court players on the same team. It does happen, however, as in the case of the Woodies (Australians Mark Woodforde and Todd Woodbridge), who were both all-around singles players. They became the most successful doubles team in the history of the game, amassing 60 doubles titles—11 of which were Grand Slam titles.

The main challenge for all-court players is specialists who can outplay them on specific surfaces. For example, the fast movers and poachers may overtake them on grass by specializing in volleying, and the hard hitters may challenge them on clay. Overall, however, they form a solid team on any surface. Table 1.4 lists some potential strengths and weaknesses of the all-court player game style.

Table 1.4 Strengths and Weaknesses of All-Court Players		
	Potential strengths	**Potential weaknesses**
SERVER	Serves and volleys effectively.	No real weakness.
SERVER'S PARTNER	Has a strong presence at the net.	No real weakness.
SERVING TEAM	Has different options for holding serve since they can generate poaching actions if required.	Can be overtaken by teams who either both stay back at the baseline to drive hard or who come in behind the return to challenge them at the net.
RECEIVER	Has many options for returns with drives, placement, and coming in behind the return.	Variations are sometimes a weakness because players may hesitate about which tactics to implement.
RECEIVER'S PARTNER	Strong presence.	No real weakness.
RECEIVING TEAM	Great potential to break serve since they have good returns, good second shots, and a receiver's partner who can apply pressure.	Can be beaten by a good serving team that uses powerful serves or poaches well, but overall doesn't have any real weaknesses.

Combined Team

A combined team pairs players with two different game styles. Doubles teams that are composed of players with different playing styles are quite common. We can identify three frequent combinations:

- Hard hitter and poacher
- Precision player and poacher
- Hard hitter and precision player

For example, at the intermediate level we often encounter an effective combination of a hard hitter who remains at the baseline to cover a lob and a quick net player who plays close to the net, ready to poach or to put a volley away.

The key for these teams is to develop an effective way of constructing the point, while respecting what each player brings to the team. Therefore, two major challenges exist for these teams:

- The first challenge is mutual respect—accepting a partner with different tactics, strengths, and weaknesses.
- The second challenge is to learn to set each other up in a way that takes advantage of the strengths of each partner.

Having different game styles is generally advantageous, since it is difficult for opponents to adjust to the dissimilar tactics of two players as they change from one position to another (server, server's partner, receiver, receiver's partner). Such diverse tactics require the opposing team to make constant adjustments from point to point.

Tables 1.5, 1.6, and 1.7 present the three most frequent combinations of game styles. The tables indicate the challenges these teams must meet when serving and receiving in order to be effective, as well as ways they must respect each other's style.

Table 1.5   Hard Hitter and Poacher Combination

	Challenges when serving	Challenges when receiving
HARD HITTER AND POACHER	Hard hitter serving • must get many first serves in to maximize his partner's strengths at the net; and • if staying back, must set up his partner with solid crosscourt, since his partner will probably be the first to intercept. Poacher serving • should be able to serve and volley without expecting his partner to poach. Should ask his partner to protect his territory well and especially to cover the lobs so that he himself is free to move in quickly after the serve. Respect • Poacher needs to accept that he does not have the best serve-and-volley partner but he does have a good receiver who can generate breaks.	Hard hitter receiving • needs to remember that he does not have to hit winners since he can set up his partner, who will move forward to intercept the server's second shot (volley or groundstroke); and • must be ready to move forward, because the server will often volley short crosscourt to avoid the receiver's partner moving forward. Poacher receiving • may not like coming in behind the return if partner positions himself at the baseline. Respect • Hard hitter needs to accept that his partner is not a powerful receiver but has great mobility and poaching actions once the point has started. • Poacher, when returning, needs to accept that his partner may at times prefer to stay back in order to use his powerful drives.

Table 1.6 Precision Player and Poacher Combination

	Challenges when serving	Challenges when receiving
PRECISION PLAYER AND POACHER	Precision player serving • must get lots of first serves in to maximize the strength of the poacher; and • should serve what the poacher prefers—either a serve to the receiver's weakness or one for which the poacher can easily anticipate the return. Poacher serving • should feel confident because her partner at the net has good volleys; and • needs to provide leadership on tactics when serving, since her partner is able to poach but often doesn't do it. Respect • Because there are fewer differences in their game styles than when one partner is a hard hitter, respect is easy to achieve. • Communication is the key to mixing up tactical situations.	Precision player receiving • must set up her partner by keeping the ball low and angled; and • if she wants to hit lobs or down-the-lines, she must let her partner know so that partner is ready to react. Poacher receiving • should be able to come in behind her return, since her partner will support her if they are involved in a volley situation against the serving team. Respect • Poacher should not force her partner to move up on the return, because the precision player is often more comfortable using her groundstroke as a second shot, to win points with accurate passing shots or lobs. • Precision player should encourage poacher to keep crossing even if she misses a few easy volleys, because it is part of the poaching game style.

Table 1.7 Hard Hitter and Precision Player Combination

	Challenges when serving	Challenges when receiving
HARD HITTER AND PRECISION PLAYER	• Both must find a way to support the server when they are struggling to hold serve, since neither has mastered poaching. Respect • Usually not a problem, because each partner will do his best to hold serve with his own game style and won't expect the other to poach a lot.	• It is a strength, as their opponent when serving will have to adapt their tactic and technique at each point to handle a power or a precision return. • The team can also keep the server's partner off balance, with the hard hitter driving down the line at times and the precision player putting up some lobs. Respect • The hard hitter must respect the precision player when the latter misses his lob or gets poached a lot, although he would prefer the precision player to hit hard crosscourt. • The precision player, who is normally consistent, must be tolerant when his partner keeps hitting hard returns even though he misses a lot. • Understanding their respective game styles is the key to supporting each other.

■ Great communication and team energy are key to double's tennis success.

All these different game styles can win tournaments if the players learn to work tactically as a team and support each other. Therefore, engage in a two-step process:

1. Identify which type of player you are and decide which tactical patterns in this manual best suit you.
2. Identify your current partner's game style. Instead of focusing on what he does not do as well as you, discover his strengths and how the two of you can work together to maximize the team performance.

2

POACHING SKILLS

Poaching is the real art of doubles. It is what every player aspires to do but often performs with only limited success. This chapter will help you understand the different types of poaches and give you specific checkpoints to facilitate your practice of each.

Although both serving and receiving teams poach, in this chapter we focus on the serving team, since this team poaches more frequently. We touch on poaching performed by the receiving team in chapters 7 and 8, when we present their different patterns of play.

Poaching is when the partner of either the server or the receiver intercepts a crosscourt shot. The player will poach if he judges the ball easy enough to do so (reaction poach), if he is sure that it will be a crosscourt shot (anticipation poach), or if the team decides in advance to do so (command or signal poach). Performing these three types of poaching well requires specific training for each.

1. Reaction—when the server's partner judges that the return is easy enough that he can cross and intercept it.

2. Anticipation—when the server's partner is sure tactically or technically that she can intercept a crosscourt shot by the receiver.

Both reaction and anticipation poaches are performed at the discretion of the net player (figure 2.1). The server is not aware of the poach in advance and must switch sides upon seeing his partner crossing to intercept.

▌ **Figure 2.1** The player crosses to poach the return, but the server is still on the same side, showing that the poach is being done per reaction or anticipation.

3. Command or signal—when the serving team decides before the point to change sides regardless of the direction of the return. The intention is agreed on verbally or communicated with hand signals.

Poaching per command requires teamwork, since both players agree to cross at the same time (figure 2.2). This move requires each player to know exactly the new area of the court he or she has to cover. A serving team typically poaches on the first serve, whereas a receiving team looks to poach per command on the return of the second serve.

Because poaching in general, performed by the serving team, reflects the ability of the server's partner to leave the area of the court he is initially covering to intercept a crosscourt return, it is necessary to first identify and train the net territory. After identifying the territory to be covered by the server's partner on a wide serve and a T serve, we will tell you how to train the serving team to do each type of poach. As mentioned earlier, we will discuss the return of serve in chapters 7 and 8; the receiver's partner also has a territory to protect and can poach per reaction, anticipation, or command against the server's first volley.

■ Figure 2.2 Both the server and his partner change sides at the same time that the receiver is hitting the ball, displaying a poach per command.

Serving Team—Territory of Server's Partner

Which returns belong to the net player? Where does the server's partner need to be positioned at the net? Does she position herself the same way regardless of serve direction (T or wide)? How much territory does she have to cover? Knowing the answers to these questions is fundamental for the net player who wants to best cover her territory, thereby applying pressure on the receiver and supporting the server.

In order to better understand the positioning and territory you should cover, or to demonstrate that territory to someone else, follow the steps as illustrated in figures 2.3 (wide serve, page 18), 2.6 (T serve, page 21), and 2.7 (whole territory, page 23) for the deuce side.

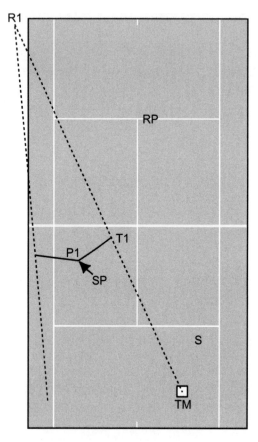

▮ Figure 2.3   The server's partner positions himself to cover the appropriate territory during a wide serve.

Wide Serve

▮ Positioning—Initially a player needs to understand where to stand to protect a good down-the-line return (see figure 2.4). You must experiment with a stepout followed by a crossover step to identify your best position at the net for covering a down-the-line return. Once you find this position, you can place a flat marker on the court to indicate where you should position yourself (P1) before the receiver hits the ball (R1).

▮ Territory—From this position (P1) you can establish your reach toward the middle, with one normal stepout and another crossover step, to intercept a crosscourt return (see figure 2.5). Position a marker at the net (T1) to identify the limit of your territory toward the middle for a wide serve.

▮ Marker to limit the territory—Finally, extend a rope from the impact point of the wide serve return (R1) over the marker (T1) to three-quarters court, where you place a marker (TM). This territory marker identifies the limit of the territory that you are responsible for (see figure 2.3). When drilling, TM helps gauge whether you are effectively covering your territory—did the ball pass inside the marker (net player's ball) or outside the marker (server's ball)?

▌ **Figure 2.4** The footwork that allows the net player to establish her position at the net and her territorial limits is difficult to visualize, but the above sequence of photographs illustrates this most important concept. These photos identify how to establish your position at the net on the deuce side against a wide serve. The process is the same for each serve location. Start by identifying where a down-the-line return would pass over the net (typically the doubles sideline), since the server's partner obviously needs to cover that shot. Knowing this point, establish (with some trial and error) where you can position yourself *(a)* to reach this shot by using a stepout action with the left leg *(b)* and a crossover with your right leg *(c)*.

■ **Figure 2.5** These three photos illustrate the concept of establishing the limit of your territory. Once the proper positioning is established to cover the down-the-line return *(a)*, perform a stepout action with the right leg *(b)* and a crossover with the left leg *(c)* to determine the extent to which you can cover a crosscourt return, and then place a marker at the net. This marker establishes the limit of your territory. The limit is different according to whether the server uses a wide serve or a T serve, because of the different angles of the possible returns (see figures 2.7 and 2.8, page 23).

T Serve

Repeat exactly the same process as for the wide serve.

- ▌ Start by covering the down-the-line return. Notice that the initial starting position (and therefore territory to cover) is modified (P2) because of the difference in trajectory between a down-the-alley return and one through the middle of the court (see figure 2.6).
- ▌ To see your limit for a crosscourt return, use the stepout and crossover footwork combination to the right, thereby identifying your right side limit (T2).
- ▌ By extending the rope from the impact point of the T serve return (R2) over the marker (T2) through to three-quarters court, you arrive at the marker (TM) that shows the limit of your territory.

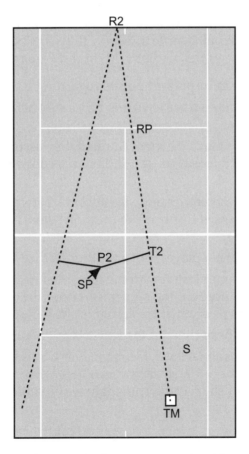

▌ **Figure 2.6** The server's partner's position for a T serve.

Whole Territory

IMPORTANT: Even if the initial position of the server's partner differs according to whether it is a wide serve (R1/P1/T1) or a T serve (R2/P2/T2), notice that territory lines converge at the same place at three-quarters court. Therefore you need only one marker (TM) to represent the territory that the net player has to cover, regardless of where the serve is hit (see figure 2.7, page 23). This point is very helpful when training or playing since the server's partner, if she does not touch the ball, can easily tell whether it was her ball by looking back to observe whether the ball passed inside or outside the marker at three-quarters court.

The distance traveled by the server's partner to cover her territory is the same on both serves. Whereas movement to the right on a T serve may seem greater, this is not the case because the initial position adopted by the net player is also farther to the right. Since the server's partner needs to choose from two different positions, she must wait for the sound of the serve to initiate her forward movement to the appropriate position for a wide serve or T serve. Regardless of the serve direction, the net player should cover any returns hit to her side of the marker (TM) at three-quarters court.

Note these three other important points regarding P1 and P2:

1. Where should the server's partner be located before moving to P1 or P2?

    ▌ The server's partner cannot immediately assume a position at P1 or P2, since the receiver could then determine the direction of the serve.

    ▌ She should therefore stand slightly back between the two markers and ready herself to move into position before the return (see figure 2.8, page 23).

2. When does the net player move to P1 or P2?

    ▌ Having communicated with the server before every point to ascertain serve direction, the server's partner moves quickly into the appropriate position at the sound of the serve.

3. How close to the net should the server's partner move for P1 and P2?

    ▌ At the professional level, the net player wants to be close to the net in position P1 or P2, since few receivers attempt lobs on the return of serve and she has the anticipation and athletic abilities to back up quickly.

    ▌ At the club level, where receivers attempt a larger number of lobs on the return, the server's partner may choose any position from the middle of the service square to the service line.

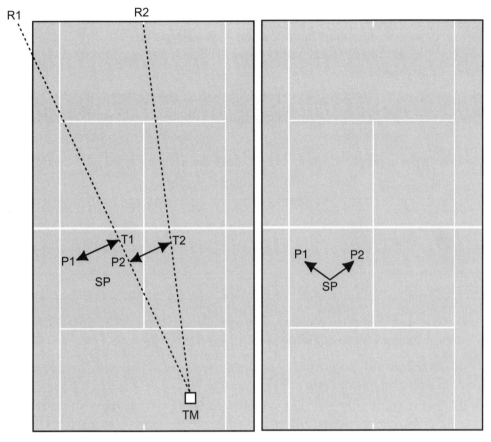

■ **Figure 2.7** Whole territory. Regardless of serving wide or T, limits of territory (T1 & T2) converge at TM at 3/4 court.

■ **Figure 2.8** Server's partner (SP) at his neutral position before moving to P1 (wide-serve) or P2 (T-serve).

Poaching When Serving— Reaction or Anticipation

■ **Poaching per reaction**—When the player can effectively protect his territory, he develops a desire to cover more shots. With this attitude he looks to cross to intercept easier crosscourt returns. The important part of poaching per reaction is that the player leaves his territory by running toward the easy ball. Understand that an easy ball is not necessarily a slower ball, since good angled slice returns are difficult to poach per reaction. More specifically, depending on his level of play, the player will seek to intercept anything from a high defensive return to a normal deep rallying shot that passes through the middle of the court.

The important part of this poaching action is for the player to quickly decide to cross or not. Therefore, in training the poach per reaction, a coach needs to vary his feeds (when returning serves) to help the server's partner recognize and call out his intention to poach (*yes*) or not (*no*). Table 2.1 shows whether the server's partner should poach per reaction on different types of returns.

Table 2.1 Poaching Decisions Per Reaction	
Type of return	**Poach per reaction?**
Various types of feeds	**Decision-making practice**
Down-the-line—hard	No (territory to cover)
Crosscourt—hard	No (too fast)
Crosscourt—angled	No (too far)
Defensive crosscourt floater	Yes
Crosscourt rally high over net	Yes

▌ **Poaching per anticipation**—Players use two types of anticipation to predict or read a crosscourt shot:

1. Technical anticipation—The server's partner reads the way the receiver is going to hit the return.

2. Tactical anticipation—The server's partner predicts from situational factors that the return will be crosscourt. For example, she notices that on a certain type of serve or on big points, the receiver always hits crosscourt.

How can you develop this ability to predict or read a crosscourt return? The returns of certain players are easy to anticipate. Tactically they always hit their slices backhand crosscourt, for example, or technically their crosscourt shots are different (impact in front and close to the body) from their down-the-line returns (impact farther away to the side). However, for a player to better assess his opponent's intention on the return, he should cultivate both types of anticipation.

Coaches can start the training of tactical anticipation by pointing out the limited possible returning options of the players. This method leads to improved technical anticipation, because players have fewer technical variations to attend to.

Five types of returns are possible in doubles:

1. Crosscourt angle
2. Crosscourt drive
3. Down-the-line drive
4. Down-the-line pass
5. Lob

▌ A well-performed poach per reaction or anticipation. The server did not know that the partner was poaching and is making an obvious effort to switch sides.

For example, imagine we are charting the types of returns done by a deuce side receiver with a big forehand and a slice backhand return.

In table 2.2, notice that *yes* is marked in four of the five return options. At first sight it may seem that the receiver has considerable variation in her returning game. However, on closer inspection it becomes clear that she only plays two types of forehand shots and two types of backhand shots. Knowing these limits, a player can more confidently use technical anticipation to determine which of the two shots the receiver will play. Even if the player cannot anticipate correctly each time, her reaction time will greatly improve since she will be deciding between two instead of five returning options.

Eliminating possibilities provides players with useful tactical information. For example, at the male professional level players rarely lob a forehand

Table 2.2	Types of First Serve Returns	
First serve return	**Forehand**	**Backhand**
Crosscourt—hard	Yes	No
Crosscourt—angled	No	Yes
Down-the-line—hard	Yes	No
Down-the-alley—pass	No	No
Lob	No	Yes

return of serve, which allows the net player to get closer to the net and be in a better position to poach if required.

Most players predominantly use two specific types of returns of serve on their forehand and backhand sides, on both the first and second serves. The reasons for such limitation are consistency and mastery of particular returns under pressure. Consider your own game. What are the typical forehand and backhand returns you use against a first serve? If you are a consistent returner, you likely mix up two returns on each side against a first serve and the same two against a second serve. If you are not a particularly steady returner, however, you may find that you are trying too many returning variations.

Remember to take some time to observe your opponents' returns. Such observations help you develop a better idea of which return to expect and therefore improve your prospects of poaching successfully.

Poaching per Command or Signal

Poaching per command or signal is achieved by coordinating (either verbally or with signs) a poaching action between the server and the server's partner. This poach is very safe since both players agree to switch at the same time. The net player tries to intercept the crosscourt return and the server covers the potential down-the-line return.

This poach is an important one to master, because it develops real team play and creates uncertainty in the receiving team. It is also useful for removing good crosscourt returns, especially the angled return.

There are three keys to success when poaching per command or signal:

1. Good communication
2. Effective disguise of the movement
3. Total understanding of the new territory to cover

▌ Professionals communicate their tactics between every point.

Communication

For good team cohesion, both players must be aware of a pending poach per command. The server's partner needs to know where the location of the serve will be (T or wide) in order to move forward to the appropriate position at the sound of the serve (see figure 2.8, page 23).

▌ Command poach—We recommend communicating the poach verbally. Players communicate verbally before a point to decide tactics, location of serve, and whether poaching will be performed. Communicating through eye contact further facilitates team bonding. Practicing together regularly helps achieve and maintain team balance more easily.

▌ Signal poach—The server's partner indicates both the location of the serve and his intention to poach or not with a hand signal behind his back (figure 2.9). The server normally verbally acknowledges seeing or agreeing with the request by saying either "okay" or "yes" or by saying "no." If he responds with "no," the server's partner gives a new signal.

▌ **Figure 2.9** The server's partner signals his intention to poach or not by placing his hand in a specific way behind his back. He can also use signals to request a specific serve location.

As shown in figure 2.10, first the server's partner signals for the location of the serve by pointing his finger to the side he wants the serve to be hit toward. The server's partner then uses his hand to indicate whether he will stay (fist) or poach (hand open).

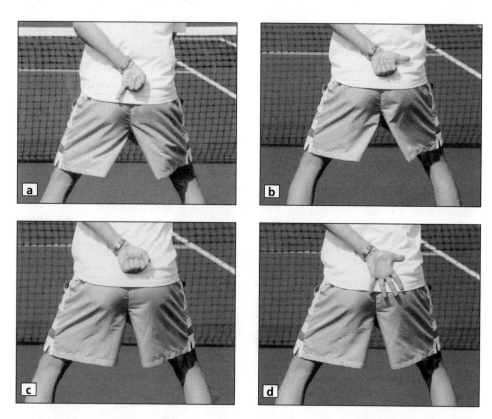

Figure 2.10 In *(a)* the little finger points to the left, which would be to the forehand of the opponent (if right-handed); the middle finger indicates a serve to the body (not shown); and in *(b)* the thumb directs the serve to the right, which would be to the backhand of the opponent (if right-handed). The server's partner then uses his hand to indicate whether he will stay *(c)* or poach *(d)*.

Disguising the Poach

In order to disguise the poach effectively, both the server and the server's partner initially move forward as usual before initiating the cross (figure 2.11). Consequently, the receiver does not read any cues that indicate a poach will be performed and will more than likely return crosscourt.

Figure 2.11   To disguise the poach, both players move initially forward after the serve and then cross to their respective positions.

Proper Positioning

Positioning is the real challenge of the poach per command and the main reason why many doubles players are reluctant to poach as much as they would like. Very few players know that the positioning and court coverage requirements change for wide and T serves, as this section will demonstrate.

When poaching against a wide serve, most players change sides and do not realize that they do not need to move farther than the middle line. As a result these players move too far or too soon. This situation becomes even more frustrating if neither member of the serving team touches the return and both players argue about whose ball it should have been. Ultimately, a lack of success leads to fewer poaching attempts.

Since the wide serve poach is critical for doubles success, we will discuss it in some depth. With regard to a poach per command, we will determine the territory of both the server and the server's partner by considering the server's territory first, since she has the greatest distance to move. After identifying what the server can cover, we will be able to determine the role of the server's partner at the net.

Poaching per Command or Signal on a Wide Serve

Poaching per command on a wide serve is the poach most misunderstood by players. They are often so unsuccessful in performing this poach that they consider only poaching against a T serve to be achievable.

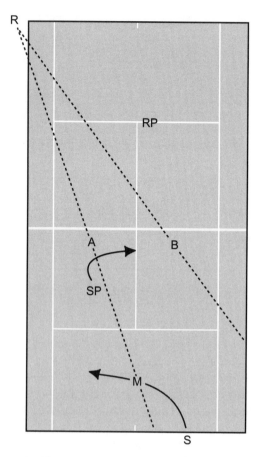

■ Figure 2.12 Poaching per command or signal on a wide serve.

The problem teams have in performing this poach successfully stems from the net player believing that he needs to change sides instead of only moving to the middle line. As a result he either moves too far, opening up the middle of the court, or he moves too soon, believing that he must rush to change sides. To understand this concept in its entirety, we will first look at how the server changes sides to cover the down-the-line return.

Server

When serving and volleying, the server needs to make the first two steps forward to disguise the poach and then quickly move to the other side to cover the down-the-line return (see figure 2.12). This quick move to the other side makes it extremely difficult to cover any ball played behind the server. We suggest that you simulate this action yourself on a tennis court and experience the limit of the balls you can volley behind you when crossing quickly to cover the down-the-line return, and place a marker (M) to identify this limit.

Having identified this limit, remember to pass a rope from the receiver's impact point (R) to M to determine where this return would pass over the net (A). The limit remains the same for a player who chooses to stay at the baseline.

Server's Partner

By establishing the limit of the server's territory, we can appreciate the extent of the territory the server's partner has to cover to his left, as indicated by marker A in figure 2.12. To his right, the territorial limit will be established by simulating an angled return with the rope and identifying where this ball would pass over the net (B).

Remember that to cover the crosscourt returns off a wide serve you do not have to change sides. Figure 2.12 demonstrates clearly that the server's partner only needs to cross to the middle line in order to cover his territory between A and B. Knowing this limit means that he does not have to rush and can wait for the bounce of the serve before moving to better disguise the poach. Also, the server's partner should cross facing the net so that he will be ready to hit either a backhand or forehand volley (figure 2.13).

■ **Figure 2.13** This sequence of a poach per command for a wide serve (both players are moving at the same time to cross) shows that the net player moves toward the middle of the court facing the net *(a-b)*. Although he is preparing to play a backhand volley *(c)*, moving in this way would allow him to just as easily play a forehand volley. To remember where to move when poaching a wide serve as a net player think, "Wide serve, White line," to move only to the center line.

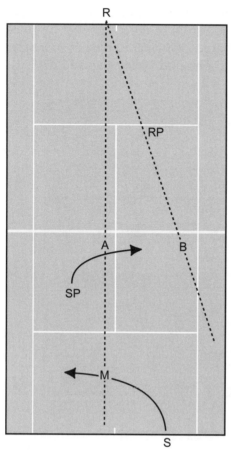

Figure 2.14 Poaching per command or signal on a T serve.

Poaching per Command or Signal on a T Serve

Applying the same method as for a wide serve, we can establish that the server who crosses on a T serve should be responsible for covering the territory indicated in figure 2.14. Since the angles of the return are not the same as those for the wide serve, the net player now has new territory to cover. Therefore the server's partner must change sides when poaching against a T serve. As in the wide serve poach, she should do so facing the net so that she is able to execute a backhand or forehand volley.

Having examined figures 2.12 and 2.14, you should be in a better position to recognize where the reluctance of many players to poach wide serves comes from. They have failed to understand the different positioning required on the two serves.

New Territory for the Net Player on the Poach per Command or Signal

As mentioned earlier, the distance the net player must travel to poach a wide serve and a T serve is essentially the same, because of the different initial positions for the two serves, as shown in figures 2.15 (wide serve) and 2.16 (T serve) on page 33. Remember that the net player should move as the serve bounces and be in the poaching position, SP 1 or 2, before the return crosses the net.

When practicing this poach, it is useful to place a flat marker at the baseline to identify to whom any through balls (balls that are not hit by either player) belong. In the pattern drill section, you will see how the poach per command can be systematically developed through a three-step progression of basket feed, live feed, and cooperative point play drills (see pages 119-122).

To gain confidence in performing the poach per command, you can start to practice it against teams who do not have powerful returns, especially those who predominantly use slice backhand returns. As you gain confidence, you

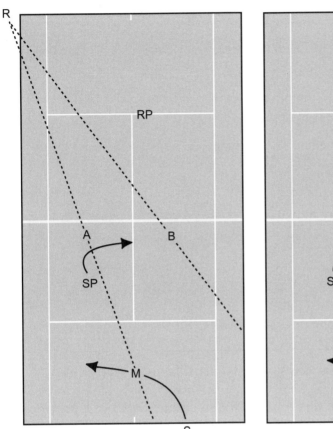 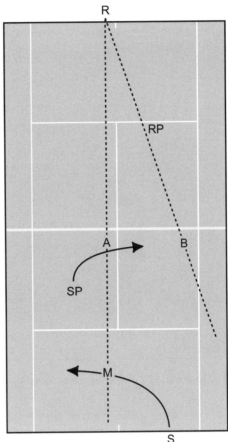

❙ Figure 2.15 Poaching per command on a wide serve, the SP moves to center line.

❙ Figure 2.16 Poaching per command on a T serve, the SP moves across the center line.

will be able to try it against more difficult returns. Ultimately you should find that holding serve really does become a team effort.

❙ Formation for the Serving Team

The I formation derives its name from the fact that the server and his partner position themselves more or less in a straight line (an "I") along the middle service line before the point begins (see figure 2.17 on page 34). By doing so, the two players can choose to move in a preplanned direction after each serve. To disguise their movements more effectively and avoid being hit by the ball, the server's partner kneels down close to the net in the middle of the court or crouches down a little farther back (see figure 2.18 on page 35). Both positions are effective and depend on personal choice.

The I formation is a variation of a command or signal poach, since the team agrees on the direction of the serve and on which side each will move

■ **Figure 2.17** The I formation showing the server and his partner in a straight line.

to. Positioning the team in this way and the subsequent options it provides can create considerable doubt in the mind of the receiver (i.e., whereas he knows the net player will move, he does not know whether it will be to the left or right).

For this variation to work most effectively, it is imperative for the server's partner to understand where he needs to position himself according to serve direction and whether the server will change sides.

■ Server stays on his side (see figure 2.19, page 36).

1. Server—The server serves and volleys on his side as usual and covers the crosscourt returns.

2. Server's partner—The server's partner at the net moves at the sound of the serve to assume his usual position to cover his territory and goes to M1 (wide serve) or M2 (T serve) (see figure 2.8, page 23).

■ Server changes sides, as in a poaching action (see figure 2.20, page 36).

1. Server—The server changes sides and takes care of the down-the-line returns.

2. Server's partner—The server's partner moves to take his poaching position toward M3 (wide serve) or M4 (T serve) (see figures 2.15 and 2.16, page 33).

▌ Figure 2.18 *(a)* Server's partner kneels down, *(b)* Server's partner crouches.

Figures 2.19 and 2.20 on page 36 show that the net player can assume four different positions (M1-M4), according to the combination of serve location (wide (R1) or T (R2)) and server intention (changing sides or not).

▌ Marker 1—This position requires the most lateral movement and should be the least used. It represents the position adopted in response to a wide serve without a crossing action.

▌ Markers 2, 3, and 4—Because the lateral movement involved is not that substantial, the server's partner does not have to rush and should at the sound of the serve move forward initially to better disguise his intended poach.

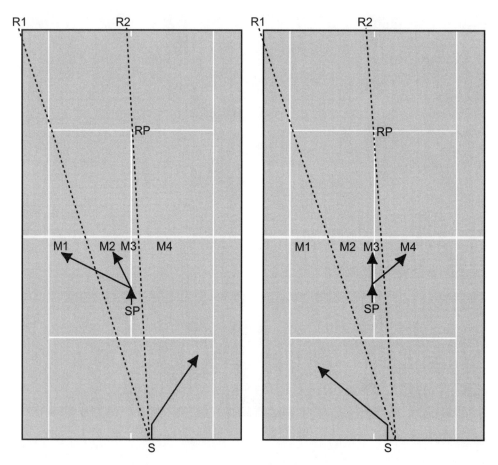

■ **Figure 2.19** I formation—server's partner's movement on wide serve to (M1) and
T serve to (M2) when server stays on his
side (No poach).

■ **Figure 2.20** I formation—server's part-
ner's movement on wide serve to (M3) and
T serve to (M4) when server changes sides
(Poach).

Serving teams use the I formation for three main reasons:

1. To put pressure on opponents, as part of the team's typical game
   style.
2. To force a receiver to return down the line when the team is struggling
   with his crosscourt return.
3. To alleviate the pressure exerted on the server's first volley by the
   movement of the receiver's partner forward.

When poaching with the I formation or poaching per command, if the
return is down the line, the server can cross and hit his second shot (volley
or groundstroke) down the line to the receiver without having the receiver's
partner in front of him trying to intercept his shot (see figure 2.21b). The

serving team should cross 70 percent of the time when using the I formation, principally in order to disrupt a good crosscourt return or to avoid the pressure of the receiver's partner; a 30 percent variation is sufficient to create uncertainty in the receiver (see figure 2.21a).

❚ Figure 2.21 *(a)* Pressure is created on the first volley when the receiver's partner moves forward after a good crosscourt return. *(b)* When the server changes sides through the I formation or poach per command, he will be able to volley down the line to the receiver without the receiver's partner in front of him looking to intercept.

The Australian Formation

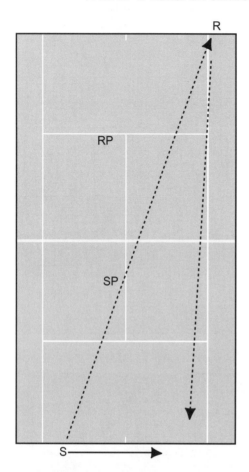

■ Figure 2.22   The Australian formation showing the server and the server's partner on the same side.

The Australian formation refers to positioning both members of the serving team on the same side at the start of a point (see figure 2.22). It is most commonly used on the advantage side of the court. The purpose of the formation is to reduce the effectiveness of the crosscourt backhand return (more often than not an angled slice) of the receiver. It forces the receiver to play down the line—typically a more difficult return. The serving team may also use it if the server prefers to hit her forehand when staying at the baseline.

The Australian formation has been superseded at the professional level by the I formation, which provides greater variation with respect to player and team movement. It can be an effective alternative at the club level, however, since players do not have to worry about disguising their poaches as they would when using the I formation.

In the Australian formation, the partner of the server starts on the same side as the server. To serve, the server may stay in her usual position (especially if she intends to stay back after her serve) to maintain the effectiveness of the serve to the backhand, or she can move closer to the middle (just as she would if intending to serve and volley). After the serve, the server tries to hit the next shot down the line back to the receiver, without having the receiver's partner in front of her.

Poaching Questionnaire

In order to improve your poaching abilities, you must increase your tactical awareness in match play. By answering a poaching questionnaire at the end of your matches, you will soon develop thought processes that will allow you to poach more often as matches progress.

Completion of the following questionnaire on the opposing team's return of serve should lead players to better poaching when serving. The serving team can complete it after a match—each question should be answered with respect to both receivers (deuce side and ad side).

POACHING QUESTIONNAIRE

Poaching per Reaction

1. Did one of the receivers often return defensively? If yes, did we poach?
2. Did we have a strong presence at the net? Did we make each receiver feel that he could not play defensively or rally balls through the middle without being intercepted?

Poaching per Anticipation

Technical anticipation

1. Were we both able to read the directional intent (crosscourt or down the line) of the forehand and backhand of the two receivers?
2. If yes, did we poach per anticipation?
3. If not, take time to replay some situations in your head to see whether you can figure it out (to see whether you can observe any changes in the receivers' body positioning, racket preparation, or impact point that suggested where they would hit).

Tactical anticipation

1. Was there a specific type of serve or situation in which one of the receivers would always return crosscourt?
2. Would one of them play safe crosscourt shots (depending on the score) that we could intercept?

Looking for tendencies

1. Which two returns did each of the receivers hit most frequently with their forehands and with their backhands?
2. Were there some returns they would never perform against certain types of serves? Did we adapt our positions accordingly?

Poaching per Command

1. How often have we poached per command compared to per reaction and anticipation?
2. Were our poaches per command well disguised or was the receiver largely hitting down the line, having seen the poach being performed?

3. Against which receiver was it easier to poach?
4. Should we have used this poach more often?

I Formation

1. Was the receiver hitting great returns?

   If yes, did we use the I formation to create uncertainty?
2. Was the receiver's partner moving forward and poaching against our first volleys?

   If yes, did we use the I formation to prevent him from doing so?
3. Should we have used it more often?

Anticipation is a skill that improves with experience and by developing the ability to analyze opponents. Refer to chapter 10 for an example of charting opponents and planning your strategies around their tactical tendencies.

PART II
SERVING TEAM

Since doubles players encounter many different types of opponents and situations, doubles teams should be trained to use the most appropriate patterns for these opponents and match situations. They must play hundreds of matches or be involved in a systematic training environment that accelerates their learning of doubles patterns.

Part II presents the most frequent movement and shot selection patterns to be mastered by the server (chapter 3), by the server's partner (chapter 4), and by both of them as a team when they are poaching or when both are at the net (chapter 5).

Remember, in order to excel in their different roles of server and server's partner, the two players need to communicate before every point. They do so for several reasons:

■ To decide what type of serve to hit. The server must vary serve characteristics (placement, speed, and spin), and the net player needs to know this information in advance—both to adapt his position at the sound of the serve and to better read cues to anticipate the return (assuming the serve goes to its intended location).

■ To determine whether the net player intends to poach. Communication allows the server to perform the appropriate crossing action to cover a potential down-the-line return.

■ To discuss tactics for countering the opposing team's returns or their second shots.

■ To keep interaction alive at all times, since mutual support is essential in a team sport.

3

SERVER PATTERNS AND DRILLS

Before we introduce the many movements and shot selection patterns for the server, we must point out the two main differences between serving in doubles and in singles:

1. Most doubles players serve and volley on the first and second serves. Tactically, net play is the name of the game and the team wants to assume this position immediately after the serve. Also, since there is no significant lateral movement to perform for the first volley, court coverage becomes easier.

Note: Players who prefer to play a groundstroke rather than a volley as their second shot stay back on both serves or only on their second serves. Because most of the professional women on the WTA tour are adopting these tactics, many coaches have decided to individualize the way they coach serving in doubles. They therefore suggest either serving and volleying or serving and staying back, depending on the playing level or strengths of each player.

2. The desired first serve percentage for doubles is 75 percent, as opposed to 60 percent in singles. It is desirable to introduce a higher percentage of first serves for two reasons. The receiver, not having to recover to the other

side of the court, can position herself inside the baseline to attack the return and can even try to move forward to the net after the return. The receiver's partner, also anticipating a better return on a second serve, is ready to move forward to put pressure on the server's first volley or groundstroke. In order to achieve a first serve percentage of 75 percent, the server must either hit hard serves to a bigger target (like the body) or use a better second serve as her first serve, placing the ball in the corners.

To hold serve, the serving team generally must create uncertainty in the receiving team so that they are kept from grooving their returns or establishing a winning tactic. The serving team accomplishes this confusion by mixing up their first serves and by including poaching actions. Thus the server has to master many different movement patterns and many different shots according to each situation.

Patterns 1 to 6 demonstrate the most common movement patterns for serve-and-volley when receiving a crosscourt return, covering a lob, and performing poaching actions. Patterns 7 to 12 highlight the server's second shot selection with either a first volley or groundstroke, according to the different positions and movements of the receiving team.

We have outlined the drills for each pattern on the deuce side, showing serve-and-volley. Players can use the same drills to train the advantage side and the option of staying back after the serve.

❚ It is common to see the server staying back after the serve on the women's pro tour.

Server's forward movement after serve

Objective

To develop the server's movement pattern toward the same court location regardless of the location of his serve and regardless of his initial position when serving.

Challenge

After a wide serve, when a server sees his partner at the net moving toward the alley to cover a potential down-the-line return, the server has a tendency to move toward the center of the court for his first volley, which makes him vulnerable to an angled return.

Execution

The server needs to anticipate where a return would pass over the net to avoid the net player. This point helps determine the territory the server must cover in moving to the net. The figures below illustrate that regardless of serve location

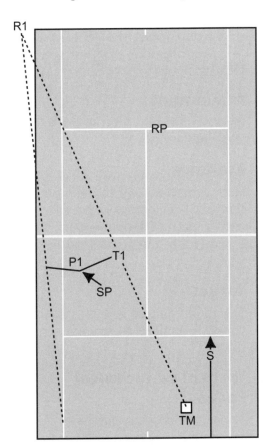

■ Server's forward movement on a wide serve.

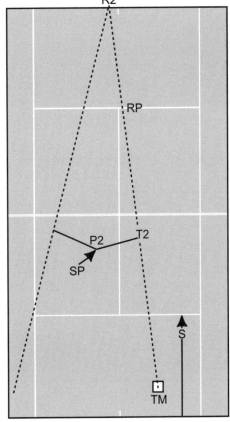

■ Server's forward movement on a T serve.

(wide or T), the trajectory of a return that avoids a net player passes the same location at three-fourths court (TM).

Consequently, the server needs to move forward to the middle of his territory, which helps him to cover any greatly angled returns.

1-1 BASKET FEED

Structure

Four players simulate a serve and forward movement to the right of the marker. Coach on the other side feeds any crosscourt returns to the right of the marker because anything to the left of the TM marker would have been intercepted by the net player.

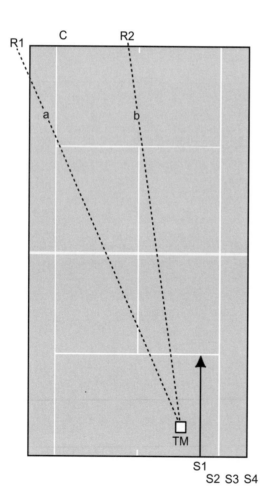

Feeds

The coach varies his feeding position from a wide serve (R1) to a T serve (R2) to reinforce the message of moving forward to the same territory regardless of the serve location.

Movement

Players move forward, using a split step before the feed.

Markers

Place a marker (TM) to define the territory limit between the server and his partner determined by line a and line b, the server's partner's limit, see page 45.

Target

The target can be any crosscourt volley, to initially encourage consistency.

Tactical or Technical Focus

Server can position differently for serving but they need to move forward in the middle of their side to better handle the return.

1-2 LIVE FEED

Structure

Three servers.
One receiver.
Coach observes the server's movement (see figure in drill 1-3, page 48).

Feeds

Server begins the drill with a serve. The return has to be hit to the right of marker TM to avoid the net player territory. If the receiver struggles, the server can either serve second serves or inform the receiver of the location of the first serve.

Movement

The server moves forward to the right of TM marker and hits a crosscourt volley.

Markers

Place a marker (TM) to define the limit of the server's territory.

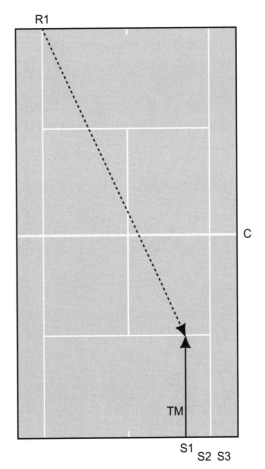

1-3 COOPERATIVE PLAY

Structure

Normal points are played.

Server

Serves and moves forward, ready for his first volley, covering the court to the right of the TM marker

Receiver

The receiver hits only crosscourt to provide repetition on the serve-and-volley.

Server's Partner

No poaching is allowed, to let the serve-and-volleyer groove his movement pattern.

Coach

Praises players' movements and ensures that points are played competitively.

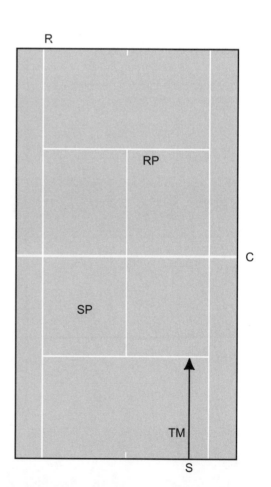

Server's crosscourt volley and recovery to middle

This pattern shows a serve-and-volley and the recovery to the middle line after performing a first volley crosscourt.

Objective

The goal of the first volley is to allow the serving team to take a good position at the net. Therefore the most frequent first volley is directed crosscourt to avoid the receiver's partner and to adopt a strong formation at the net against the baseline drive or lob. Thus the server, after playing her first volley crosscourt, recovers quickly to the middle of the court to assume the proper team positioning when both are at the net.

Challenge

To know where to recover and to do so before the receiver's second shot.

Execution

Players need to comprehend the territory each player must protect when they are both at the net and the position each player must take. Coaches can help players understand these territories by illustrating the down-the-line and angled passing shot options for the receiver's second shot on a diagram or with ropes on the court. The middle of this angle should then be determined and a marker (M) or a rope should be positioned to make each player fully aware of the territory she must cover. The server will then understand why she has to recover to the middle of the court instead of staying in her half-court, as many intermediate players do.

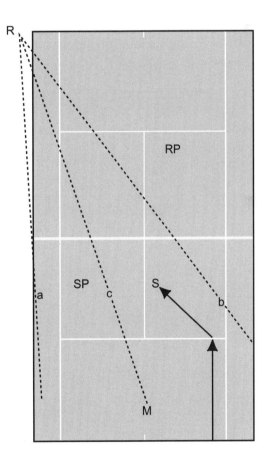

■ Territories of server and server's partner after server's first volley crosscourt. Line a = down-the-line; Line b = angled crosscourt; Line c = the middle of the territory between the two extreme possibilities. These lines determine the territories the server and server's partner must cover when both are at the net.

2-1 BASKET FEED

Structure

Four players on one side of the court rotate as server.
The coach feeds returns from the opposite side of the court.

Feeds

The coach uses two balls. She simulates a return so that the server can play a first volley. She then returns the ball and gives feedback on whether the server recovered in time and effectively covered the territory.

Movement

Players move forward for the first volley (generally around the service line), recover to the middle for the second volley (M2), and move to the back of the line.

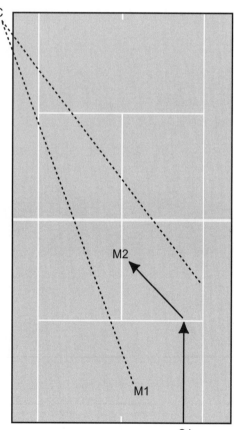

Markers

Marker 1 defines the limit of the server's territory after doing a crosscourt volley.

Marker 2 identifies where the player should recover after the first volley.

Target

Server hits a deep crosscourt volley.

Tactical or Technical Focus

The server needs to recover to the middle of the court before the receiver executes his second shot to handle either the angled shot or the drive down the middle.

2-2 LIVE FEED

Structure

Two servers—rotate after each serve.
Two receivers—rotate after every two returns.

Receivers

Return crosscourt. Their second shot can be played anywhere in the server's territory (i.e., to the right of the dotted line (M1), represented by a rope or markers on the ground).

Servers

Move forward for their first volley and recover to the center line (M2), to execute their second volley.

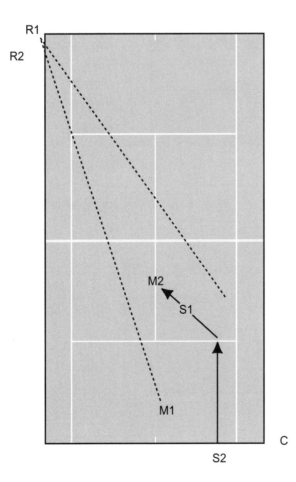

2-3 COOPERATIVE PLAY

Structure

Normal points are played.

Server

Serve and deep crosscourt volley, followed by a quick recovery to the middle of the court.

Receiver

Can only hit crosscourt and must stay back to let the server practice a deep crosscourt volley and give him time to recover to the middle.

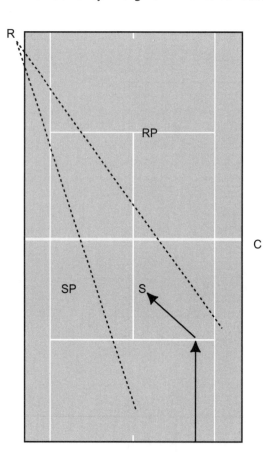

Server's Partner

No poaching.

Receiver's Partner

Does not attempt to poach in order to let the server volley crosscourt and recover to the middle.

Coach

Praises players' movements and speed in recovering before the second shot. Ensures the competitiveness of all players.

Server sprints to net to put away floaters

Objective

This pattern trains players to be ready to put away high defensive returns (floaters) by moving in close to the net and punching the volley down the line at the receiver's partner, or by angling it away from both players.

Challenge

Most servers expect their partners to intercept floater returns and therefore do not react quickly enough to contact the volley above the net and play it aggressively. Some players also have the tendency to wait for these returns, stopping their forward progressions with their split steps. The challenge for the server therefore becomes to commit to moving forward aggressively, closing in to the net.

Execution

The coach should set up the drills to challenge both players' decision-making abilities and the speed with which they sprint toward the net, by interspersing drive and floater returns.

3-1 BASKET FEED

Structure

Four players in the role of server take turns simulating serve-and-volley. The coach is on the other side. The goal of this drill is to improve decision making and train specific movement patterns.

Feeds

The coach mixes drive (line a) and floater (line b) returns from a wide serve position. The coach will repeat the same drill from different return positions.

Movement

Server is ready to stop in order to handle a difficult return at M1, or sprint up close to the net at M2 to put the floater away.

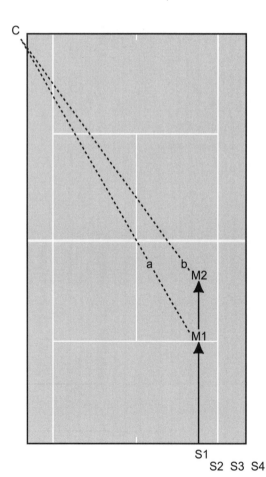

Markers

Place marker M1 on the service line to encourage players to move forward quickly for drive returns. Place marker M2 close to the net to encourage sprinting to the net to put away floaters.

Target

The server should direct his volley down the line on high floaters and angle it crosscourt when the return is lower.

Tactical or Technical Focus

Encourage players to use a key word like "go" when they identify a floater, to help them focus on the task.

Because a floater is relatively high over the net, work on improving the pace they can generate with the volley (i.e., by using a punch volley) on the forehand and backhand sides.

54

3-2 LIVE FEED

Structure

Two servers—alternating serves.
Two receivers—rotating every two returns.

Feeds

Mix crosscourt drives and floaters. If the serve is too difficult for the receiver, he can request the type of serve he would like to receive.

Movement

Server is ready to stop in order to handle a difficult return at M1, or to sprint up close to the net at M2 to put the floater away.

Markers

Place marker M1 on the service line to encourage players to move forward quickly for drive return. Place marker M2 close to the net to encourage sprinting to the net to put away floaters.

Decision

Players can still use the word "go" when identifying the floater.

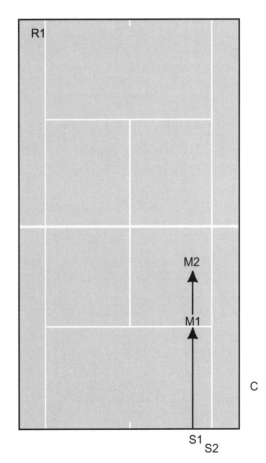

3-3 COOPERATIVE PLAY

Structure

Normal points are played.

Server's Partner

No poaching is allowed, to ensure that the server works his movement and first volley.

Receiver

Keeps varying the crosscourt returns but continues to provide a majority of floaters.

Coach

The coach attends to the server's speed of reaction, appropriateness of decision making, and the quality of their volley execution.

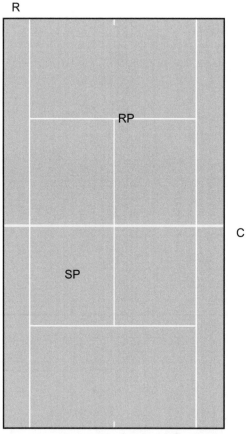

Server changes sides to intercept lobs

Objective

On the return, if the server's partner is successfully lobbed over, the server needs to change sides to intercept the lob in the air. In this way she is able to avoid chasing the ball back and to better maintain an attacking team formation by recovering back to the net.

Challenge

The main challenge is to react to the lob over your partner. Therefore the training needs to include receiving a return crosscourt to be played with a volley and a lob over your partner to have you react and cross over to intercept with a smash. To master the shot selection on the backhand smash or conventional overhead.

Execution

• Deuce side—The server crosses behind her partner to play a backhand smash. Because the backhand smash is not as powerful as a conventional overhead, it is played back down the line to the receiver. This move allows the server to reposition herself to play out the point. The server's partner changes sides and backs up toward the service line.

• Ad side—On this side, it is easier for the server to cross behind her partner and play a conventional overhead. The server has the option to smash crosscourt at the receiver's partner at the service line, between the two players, or down the line at the receiver. The server's partner changes sides and backs up toward the service line to give her partner space to smash anywhere and to be ready to maintain the attacking position.

Note: The following drills on deuce side address the backhand smash.

4-1 BASKET FEED

Structure

Four players on one side rotate in server's position.
The coach on the other side, feeds a down-the-line lob (line a) or a crosscourt drive (line b).

Feeds

The coach simulates a return by dropping a ball on the ground and hitting a groundstroke. At the beginning, the coach feeds only a lob to develop the skill of changing sides and smashing. Once successful, he trains the reaction and decision of the server by alternating down-the-line lobs and crosscourt drives.

Server

Needs to change sides and look to recover quickly toward the net after the backhand smash.

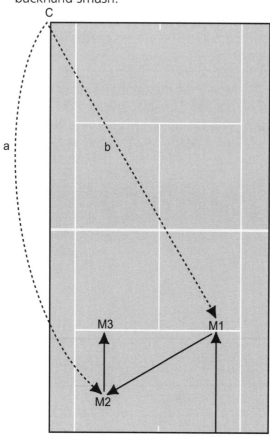

Markers

Place a flat marker at the service line (M1) so that the server moves up to this line despite knowing that a lob will be fed to her. M2 indicates where the server should smash from. Place another flat marker to remind the server of the forward recovery (M3) after playing the backhand smash.

Target

Direct the backhand smash down the line to the receiver.

Tactical or Technical Focus

Perform the backhand smash by keeping the elbow up until impact. Even if the backhand smash is not powerful, it is better to intercept the lob and keep the net advantage.

4-2 LIVE FEED

Structure

Like drill 4-1, except three players serve and one player returns.

Feeds

Three players take turns serving.
One player returns a down-the-line lob (line a) or a crosscourt drive (line b).

Markers

M1, at the service line, indicates the location to which the server should move or hit the first volley from if the return is crosscourt.
M2 represents the location where the server should hit his backhand smash from. M3 indicates the area the server should recover to after the smash.

Target

Direct the backhand smash down the line toward the receiver.

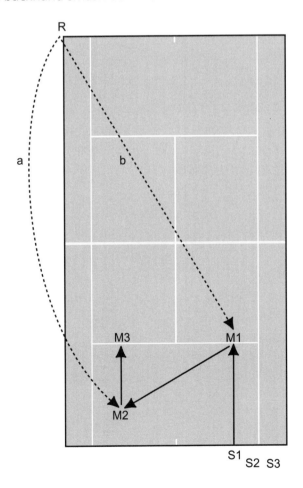

4-3 COOPERATIVE PLAY

Structure

Normal playing situation from deuce side.

Server

Needs to reach M1, even if anticipating the lob.

Receiver

Varies returns between the lob (75 percent) and the crosscourt drive (25 percent).

Server's Partner

Remains very passive, allowing the lob to go over her head so that the server can practice her backhand smash or first volley (i.e., the partner does not poach or cover the lob).

Note: In a match, the server will experience difficulties with the crosscourt return if she does not move quickly to cover it. Similar problems will arise with the lob if she does not do her split step.

Server changes sides to chase lob returns

The server may find himself chasing down the lob if for some reason he was wrong-footed or thought that his partner was going to take it.

Objective

Having chased the lob, the server must be able to defend with an effective lob in reply. However, because opponents can come to expect the lob, the server must be able to intersperse lobs with a few drives or angled replies.

Challenge

To react and run quickly to chase down the lob and then to select the most appropriate tactical response to the lob return.

Execution

• Server's partner—Changes sides and moves to the baseline in anticipation that the server will lob in reply. At the baseline he will be better positioned to retrieve the probable smash by their opponents.

• Opponents—When the receiver sees his lob bouncing behind the net player, he moves toward the net to join his partner, expecting and preparing to put away the defensive shot (lob) of the server.

5-1 BASKET FEED

Structure

Four servers.
The coach is on the opposite side of the court.

Feeds

At the beginning the coach feeds only a lob to develop the skill of chasing the lob. Once successful, he trains the reaction and decision of the server by alternating down-the-line lobs (line a) and crosscourt drives (line b).

Server

Move to M1 to be ready to volley or to chase the lob.

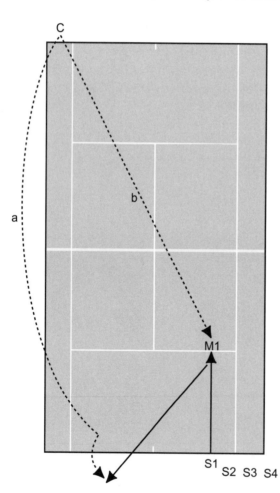

Markers

Place a flat marker at the service line (M1) so that the server moves up this line to play the crosscourt return or to chase the down-the-line lob.

Target

After a lob, the server plays a deep backhand lob, then (when possible) hits a drive or angles a shot low over the net. After a crosscourt return, the server volleys crosscourt.

Tactical or Technical Focus

Decide whether a backhand lob or backhand drive is appropriate in reply to the lob return.

5-2 LIVE FEED

Structure

Three servers on one side.
One returner mixing crosscourt drives and down-the-line lobs.

Server

Serve and volley moving towards M1 to handle crosscourt drive returns (line b).
If there is a lob (line a), let it bounce before answering with a lob or drive.

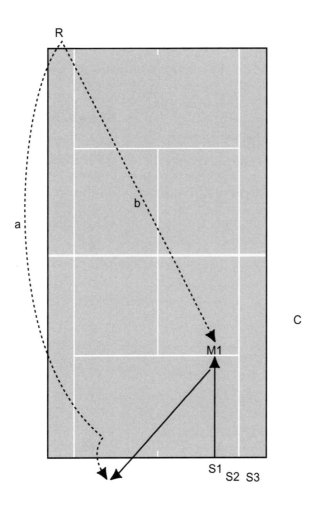

5-3 COOPERATIVE PLAY

Structure

Normal points are played.

Server

In reply to a return crosscourt, the server volleys crosscourt and plays out the point. In reply to a lob return, the server moves back (line a), letting the lob bounce, and practices the different replies—lob, drive, and angle.

Server's Partner

Passive—no poaching, no covering of lobs.

Note: When being lobbed, the server's partner needs to recover to the baseline (line b) in anticipation of his partner's defensive lob.

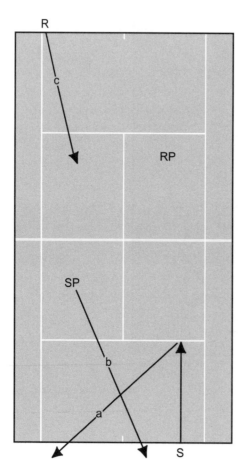

Receiver

Lobs 75 percent of the time. Comes to the net after the lob bounces (line c).

Server changes sides when partner poaches

Objective

The server must change sides quickly when he sees his partner crossing to poach per reaction or anticipation.

Challenge

Too often the server thinks that his partner will finish the point when he poaches. Unfortunately, such is not always the case. The server must therefore discipline himself to change sides, even if her partner has an easy ball to poach, in order to cover the open court.

Execution

The diagram on page 66 illustrates the server's decision to change sides when his partner is poaching per reaction or anticipation.

6-1 BASKET FEED

Structure

Coach as the receiver.
Three players as servers.
One player as the server's partner.

Server's partner

Mixes up movements, poaching half of the time, to train the server's reaction to changing sides.

Coach

Feeds

- Crosscourt floater (line a): to trigger the poach per reaction by the server's partner or the closing in of the server.

- Crosscourt drive (line b): where a poach per anticipation is required or a challenging first volley for the server.

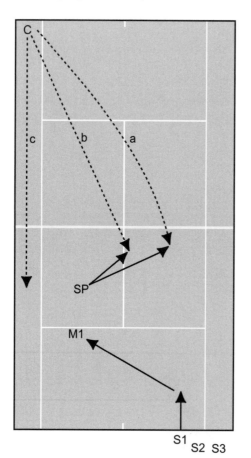

- To the open court (line c), when the server's partner poaches the return.

Server

Simulates a serve and moves in ready to do a first volley crosscourt if the server's partner does not poach per reaction or anticipation, or crosses quickly to the open court as soon as he sees his partner poaching to cover the down-the-line shot (line c) fed by the coach.

6-2 LIVE FEED

Structure

Coach as the receiver.
Two players as servers.
Two players as the server's partner.

Server

Serves and volleys.

Server's Partner

Mixes up movements, poaching half of the time, to train the server's reaction to changing sides.

Coach

Does a live feed by returning the serve and will basket feed a second shot down the line, into the open court, when the server's partner poaches per reaction or anticipation.

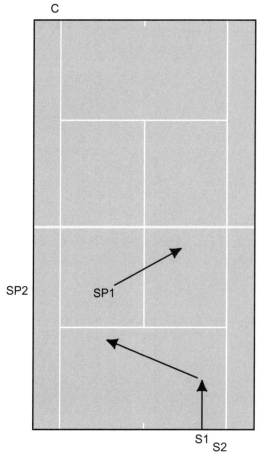

6-3 COOPERATIVE PLAY

Structure

Normal points are played.

Server

Changes sides, just as she would in a match when her partner poaches per reaction or anticipation.

Receiver

Returns crosscourt.

Server's Partner

Poaches 50 percent of the time. This will keep the server alert between hitting his first volley and changing sides as soon as the poach is initiated. Try to win the point when he poaches.

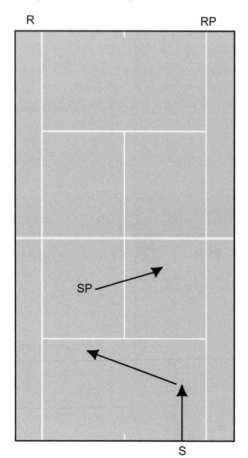

Receiver's Partner

Positioned at the baseline to increase the chances of continuing the point.

Shot Selection Patterns for the Server's First Volley or Groundstroke

Following the serve, the server has two options—to serve and volley (which is most common) or to serve and stay back. Regardless of which decision he makes, if the return is crosscourt the server needs to play a first volley or groundstroke that is specific to the game situation.

There are six possible positions and movements of the receiving team that influence the server's tactical decision about which type of first volley or groundstroke to play. Table 3.1 illustrates these six different combinations of the receiving team's positions and how the server should respond to each.

Table 3.1 Receiving Team's Positions and Server's Responses			
RECEIVING TEAM'S POSITIONS AND MOVEMENTS		**SERVER'S SECOND SHOT OPTIONS**	
Receiver	**Receiver's partner**	**1st volley**	**1st groundstroke**
Baseline	Service line	Deep crosscourt shot	Deep crosscourt shot
Moving forward	Service line	Short crosscourt shot	Short crosscourt shot
Baseline	Moving forward	Angle or down-the-line	Angle, lob, or down-the-line
Baseline	Poaching	Down-the-line	Down-the-line
Baseline	Baseline	Any shot hit down the middle or to weakness	Any shot hit down the middle or to weakness
Moving forward	Moving forward	Angle or lob	Drive middle, angle, lob

Note: The patterns will cover both of the server's options— to serve and volley (first volley) or serve and stay back (groundstroke)—since these possibilities are used from club to professional level. The drills and the pattern titles will illustrate only the serve-and-volley options.

Server's first volley—deep crosscourt

We will start with the most frequent receiving team position at club level, which is the receiver staying back after the return while his partner remains at the service line.

Objective

This pattern teaches servers to perform a first volley or groundstroke deep crosscourt to the receiver. Such a play provides a difficult second shot for the receiver. Since the receiver hits the shot far from the net, either the server gains a good net position after a serve-and-volley, or if the server stays back, the server's partner gains a good opportunity to poach the receiver's second shot.

Challenge

To execute a good second shot after the serve when the returns are fast, low, or angled.

Execution

The tactic itself is simple, but the implementation is difficult since the return comes with many variations. Therefore, specific drills that mix up the returns are important for training this most common pattern for initiating the point in doubles.

Note: We outline here the drills for the serve-and-volley, which is the most recommended tactic for advanced doubles. You can reproduce the same model of drills for players staying back.

7-1 BASKET FEED

Structure

Four players rotate as server.
The coach is on the other side of the court to train with basket feeding.

Feeds

Return feed—The coach simulates returns from the baseline (wide or T), mixing up low returns and drive returns. The coach should adapt the feed to the level of the players.
Second shot feed—After the server hits the first crosscourt volley at M1, the coach feeds a second ball for the server to volley at M2 (pattern 2, pages 49-52).

Movement

Server moves forward toward M1 to execute first volley and recovers quickly to M2 for the second volley.

Target

First volley—deep crosscourt.
Second volley—anywhere.

Tactical or Technical Focus

Practicing a first volley on low and fast returns.

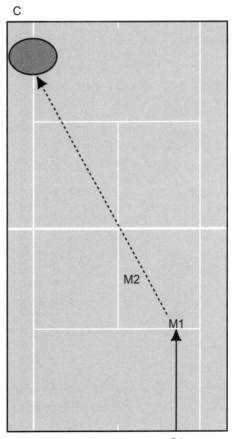

7-2 LIVE FEED

Structure

Similar to drill 7-1, but server serves to better simulate and prepare for match play.

Four players rotate as server.

The coach is on the other side of the court to return serves.

Feeds

Return feed—The coach returns from the baseline (wide or T), mixing up low returns and drive returns. The coach should adapt the return to the level of the players.

Second shot feed—After the server hits the first crosscourt volley at M1, the coach feeds a second ball, or hits back to the server, to volley at M2.

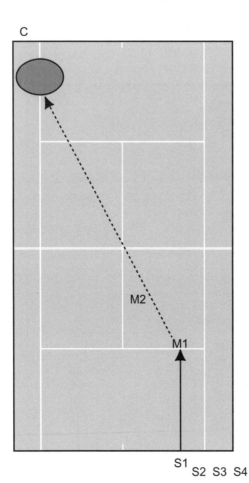

C

M2

M1

S1 S2 S3 S4

Movement

Server moves forward toward M1 to execute first volley and recovers quickly to M2 for the second volley.

Target

First volley—deep crosscourt.
Second volley—anywhere.

Tactical or Technical Focus

Practicing serve-and-volley on low and fast returns.

As players rotate, hitting one serve each, the coach or another player returns the serve.

Note: If the receiver struggles with the return, the server can signal the location of his serve or hit only second serves.

7-3 COOPERATIVE PLAY

Structure

Normal points are played.

Server

First volley is deep crosscourt and recovery is to the middle of the court.

Receiver

Returns crosscourt.

Server's Partner

No poaching is allowed.

Receiver's Partner

Stays at service line so that no additional pressure is applied to server's first volley.

Coach

If appropriate the coach should provide feedback while players are grooving this classic serve-and-volley drill.

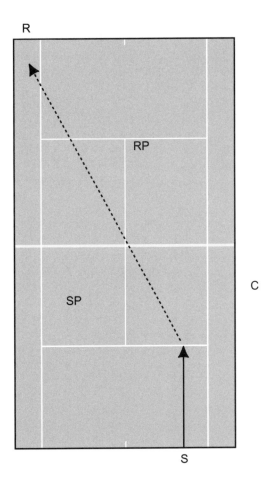

Server's first volley—short crosscourt angle

When the receiver moves in behind her return and her partner remains at the service line, the server must learn to use a short crosscourt angled shot. This situation usually occurs on a weak or high bouncing second serve when the receiver has moved inside the baseline, ready to attack. The receiver can chip and charge or drive and charge.

Objective

The server should play an angled shot rather than playing it deep, because a deep shot would provide the incoming receiver with an easier volley to hit. This angled volley or angled passing shot forces the receiver to volley up. The serving team is then ready to attack.

Challenge

The use of angled approach volleys is not common to singles play and therefore requires specific practice. Recognizing that the receiver actually comes in and understanding that playing a safe crosscourt volley is likely to spell trouble are important elements. The server must also develop a good feel (sometimes called good hands) for taking the pace off the ball and redirecting the return. Start with the chip-and-charge situation. The chip shot provides the server with a slower return to negotiate with the first volley or the passing shot. Then progress to the drive-and-charge scenario.

8-1 BASKET FEED

Structure

Four players rotate as server.
The coach simulates, through basket-feeding, a return of serve to develop the pattern.

Feeds

The coach adapts the feeds to the level of the players and mixes up chip-and-charge and drive-and-charge returns to simulate match play.

Movement

Each player in turn serves one ball, moves in to M1 to volley the ball that the coach basket feeds, and then recovers toward M2 before the ball bounces (since the receiver would have volleyed it).

Target

The first volley is played as a short crosscourt angle.

Tactical or Technical Focus

The server will need most of the time to have a technique where he takes the pace of the ball to angle effectively. After the angle volley, the receiver will have to volley up, and the serving team needs to be ready to put the next volley away.

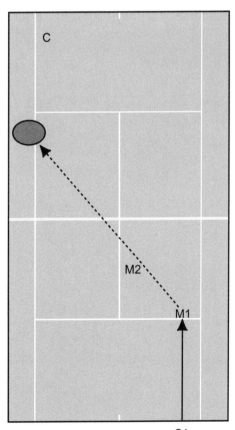

8-2 LIVE FEED

Structure

Two servers rotate, serving one second serve each.
Two receivers mix up chip-and-charge and drive-and-charge returns.

Server

Practices angled first volley and recovers to M2.

Feeds

If the receiver struggles with the return, the server can indicate the location of the second serves.

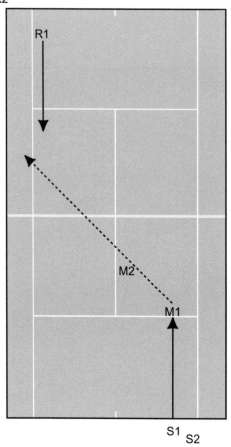

Movement

Players rotate after the server has played a specified number of successful volleys, or after a designated amount of time.

Target

The server tries to play a given number of successful angled volleys.

8-3 COOPERATIVE PLAY

Structure

Normal points are played.

Server

Angles first volley and recovers quickly to the middle.

Receiver

Is forced to come in behind the return of second serves.

Server's Partner

Is not allowed to poach the return.

Coach

Can provide any type of feedback.

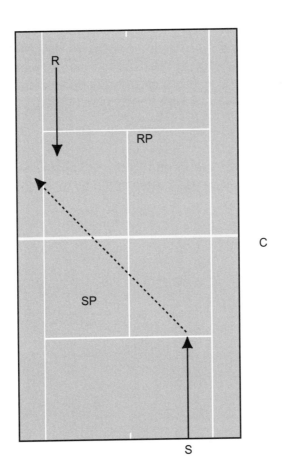

Server's first volley—angle and down-the-line shots

When the receiver's partner moves forward and the receiver stays back, the server must respond with appropriate second shots. This situation occurs commonly with a good receiving team. The receiver's partner is ready to put pressure on the server whenever he sees the server encountering difficulty with a low return while volleying or with a deep return while staying back after the serve.

Objective

• Volley—The server must learn to take the pace off the ball for an angled volley or to open the wrist at the last second for redirecting the ball toward the alley. In playing this type of touch volley, the server has to prepare with his racket out in front. He must learn to be alert so that he can play a second volley down the line if the opponent hits his first one back.

• Groundstroke—The server seeks to hit very powerfully or to hit accurately away from the net players.

Challenge

In this situation, the server needs to volley to the alley or angle the shot crosscourt to avoid presenting the receiver's partner with an easy first volley. These two types of first volleys are obviously never performed in singles play, which is one of the reasons why singles players often struggle to hold serve in doubles.

Execution

If the server stays back, executing this play is like doing a passing shot, since the rallying shot would be easily intercepted by the net player.

9-1 BASKET FEED

Structure

Four players rotate as server.
The coach is on the other side of the court.

Feeds

The coach feeds challenging crosscourt returns.

Movement

Each player serves one ball and moves in to M1 to either volley an angle and recover to M2, or volley down the line and recover to M3.

Target

Players aim first volley down the line to the alley (line a) or angled crosscourt (line b).

Tactical or Technical Focus

To master volleys, in particular the volleys to the alley that are not played in singles.

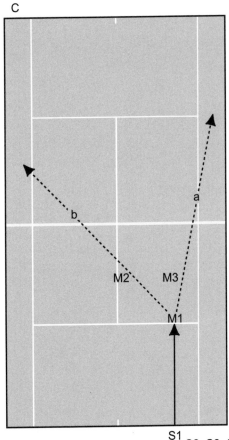

9-2 LIVE FEED

Structure

Four players rotate serving and volleying.
The coach is on the other side of the court returning serves.

Feeds

The coach hits challenging crosscourt returns.

Movement

Each player serves one ball and moves in to M1 to either volley an angle and recover to M2, or volley down the line and recover to M3.

Target

Players aim first volley down the line to the alley or angled crosscourt.

Tactical or Technical Focus

To master volleys, in particular the volleys to the alley, that are not played in singles.

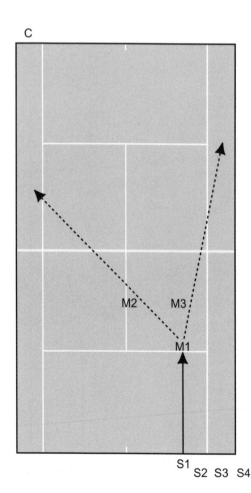

9-3 COOPERATIVE PLAY

Structure

Normal points are played.

Server

Practices to avoid the pressure of the receiver's partner moving forward with angled and down-the-alley volleys.

Receiver's Partner

Moves forward regardless of the quality of the return, since the practice is geared toward the server.

Receiver

Returns crosscourt and stays at the baseline after the return.

Server's Partner

Is not allowed to poach the return but needs to recover toward midcourt just in case the receiver's partner returns the server's first volley (see pattern 16, pages 101-103).

Coach

Even when the players are playing points, the coach can use some key words to help the players refocus on the teaching points received during the basket feed drill.

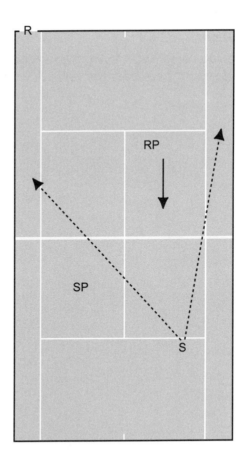

Server's first volley—down the line

The server must learn how to respond when the receiver's partner poaches. This pattern usually occurs when the receiver has played a good return that has forced the server to be defensive. The receiver's partner, anticipating a weak crosscourt shot, poaches to intercept the volley or the groundstroke.

Objective

The server must be aware of the opponent's poach and respond by playing a shot down the line.

Challenge

The server must not be distracted by this tactic, but must stay calm. She must change her decision at the last second, when she sees the poach, to redirect her volley down the line. Players must understand that even playing a volley crosscourt against a well-timed poach does not guarantee that they will lose the point. They can even view it as an opportunity to win the point outright with a down-the-line volley.

Execution

By keeping her racket in front, the server can more easily lay her wrist back at the last second to redirect the volley down the line.

10-1 BASKET FEED

Structure

Four players rotate as server.
The coach is on the other side of the court.

Feeds

The coach challenges the server with crosscourt feeds that simulate the difficult returns on which the receiver's partner would normally poach.

Movement

Each player in turn serves one ball, moves in to M1 to play the down-the-line first volley, and then recovers to M2.

Target

The server aims the first volley down the line.

Tactical or Technical Focus

By keeping your racket in front of you, it is easier to open the wrist slightly and redirect the volley down the line with disguise.

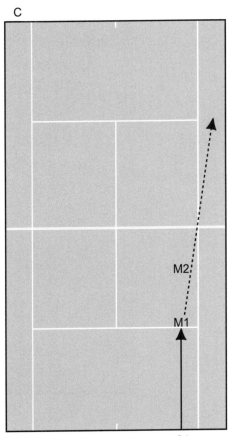

10-2 LIVE FEED

This drill focuses on decision making.

Structure

Two players serve and volley.
One player returns crosscourt.
One player practices as the receiver's partner alternating between poaching and not poaching.

Note: The point is not played out. Players concentrate on making the right decisions and executing them accordingly.
The server should play down the line if the receiver's partner poaches. Otherwise she should volley crosscourt.

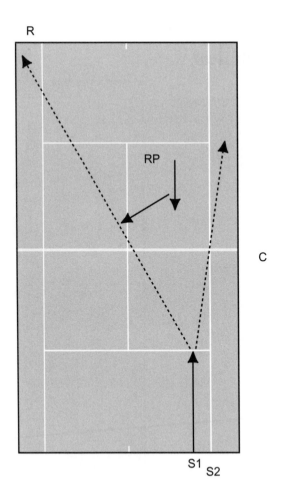

10-3 COOPERATIVE PLAY

Structure

Normal points are played.

Server

Hits first volley down the line if the receiver's partner poaches and hits cross-court if she does not.

Receiver

Returns aggressively and stays at the baseline after the return, changing sides when he sees his partner poaching.

Server's Partner

Is not allowed to poach the return.

Receiver's Partner

Moves forward and poaches 50 percent of the time.

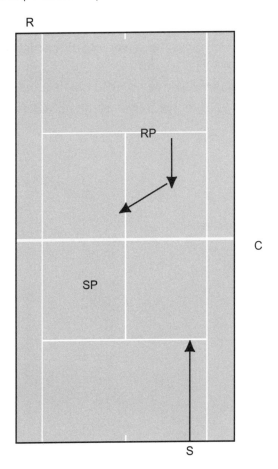

Server's first volley—to opponent's weakness

The server plays to the opponent's weakness or to the middle when the receiving team is positioned with both players back. The receiving team often adopts this formation in an effort to win more points when they cannot return effectively.

Objective

The server must choose from two options with his first volley or ground-stroke:

1. Exploit the weakest shot of either the receiver or receiver's partner.
2. Volley down the middle to isolate one player and play back behind him.

Challenge

In the absence of pressure from an opposing net player, the server often relaxes too much or plays too safe a volley and thus presents the receiving team with an easy ball to attack. The server should therefore continue to use the first volley with a view to winning the point as quickly as possible.

Drills

- The basket feed drill gives the server lots of practice at placing the first volley where he wants it to go.
- The live feed drill develops the reflex to isolate a player.
- Cooperative play allows the server to practice serving where he prefers.

11-1 BASKET FEED

Structure

Four players rotate as server, each simulating a serve.
The coach is on the other side of the court.

Feeds

The coach varies his crosscourt returns to provide good training on the first volley.

Movement

Each player in turn moves in toward M1 to volley and then recovers according to his shot selection.

Target

The server practices playing his first volley toward four different targets, each representing a possible groundstroke weakness. The coach calls the target before the player simulates a serve.

Tactical or Technical Focus

To develop the server's accuracy in placing the first volley.

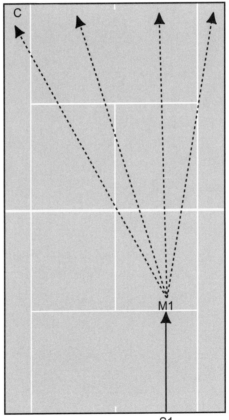

11-2 LIVE FEED

Structure

Three players rotate as server.
The coach (as receiver) and one player (in the role of receiver's partner) are on the other side of the court.

Feeds

Each server feeds a first volley to the middle. The coach or his partner hits the ball back to the server, who has to volley back to the same receiving player who returned it.

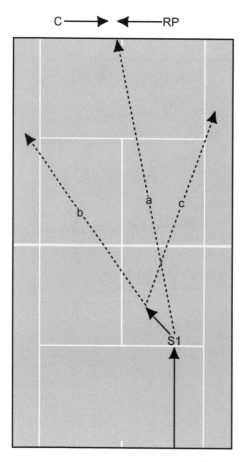

Target

First volley in the middle (line a). Second volley behind the player that just hit it (line b if receiver, or line c if receiver's partner).

Tactical focus

To improve server's shot selection.

11-3 COOPERATIVE PLAY

Structure

Normal points are played, during which the serving team decides which tactics to use against a receiving team that stays back.

Server

Hits first volley deep, to a specific stroke of the receiver, or down the middle.

Receiver

Returns crosscourt and stays at the baseline after the return.

Server's Partner

Is not allowed to poach the return and will implement the same pattern of isolating the opponent who hit the ball.

Receiver's Partner

Stays on the baseline for the return to play both back tactics.

Coach

Can specify different tactics to ensure variation.

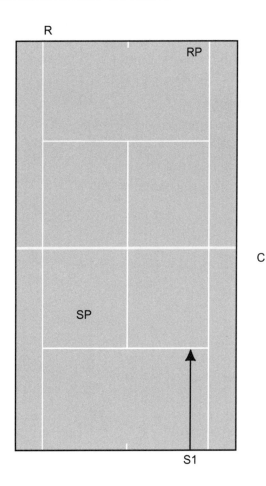

Server's first volley—angle or lob shots

The server must learn to perform either an angle or a lob when the two members of the receiving team are moving in. This situation usually happens after a weak second serve; the receiver moves in and her partner moves forward too. Such movements create considerable pressure on the server's second shot (volley or groundstroke).

Objective

When volleying, the server's first choice is to angle her volley to avoid the pressure of both receiving players. Her second choice (which she should use only as a variation since it is a difficult shot) is a lob volley, when the receiver's partner is too close to the net. When staying back, the server should choose according to her game style whether she prefers to drive hard crosscourt (since the receiver will not yet be close to the net) or to angle a precise passing shot. She can also choose at times to lob the receiver's partner, when the latter moves close to the net.

Challenge

To remain focused on the objective of playing angles or lobs and not to be distracted by the incoming opponents.

12-1 BASKET FEED

Structure

Three players rotate as server.
The coach and one player (as receiver's partner) are on the other side of the court.

Feeds

After the server simulates a serve-and-volley by moving to M1, the coach (who is the receiver) feeds a low return and comes to the net.

Movement

The coach simulates the receiver coming in and the receiver's partner moves in very close to the net to train the server to hit an angle (line a) or lob volley (line b). For safety reasons during the drill, if the lob is not done well, the receiver's partner will make the volley or smash in the open court and not back at the server. The server moves to M2 after hitting an angle volley or to M3 after hitting a lob volley.

Tactical or Technical Focus

The lob needs to surprise the receiver's partner, therefore prepare for an angle volley and at the last second execute the down-the-line lob.

Note: We have not included a live feed drill for this pattern, to point out that the three-step drill progression is not always necessary. On the other hand, a live feed drill does ensure a good transition between the basket feed and the actual playing situation.

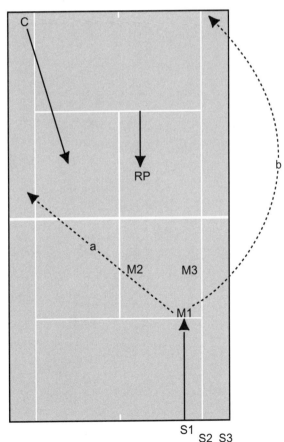

12-2 COOPERATIVE PLAY

Structure

Normal points are played.

Server

Hits only second serves to allow the receiver to come in. Needs to vary the use of angled (line a) and lob volleys (line b).

Receiver

Comes in with chip-and-charge or drive-and-charge.

Server's Partner

Is not allowed to poach the return. Moves back toward the service line after the crosscourt return, noticing the pressure applied by the receiving teams.

Receiver's Partner

Moves forward.

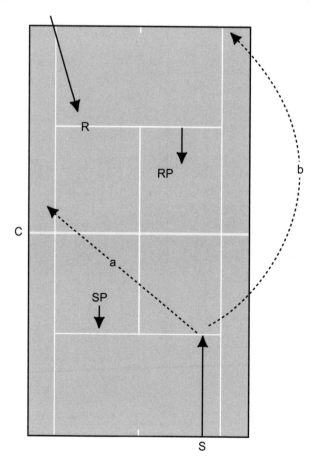

4

SERVER'S PARTNER PATTERNS AND DRILLS

The server's partner is often the key player in helping the team to hold serve consistently. Her first role is to position herself so that she can cover the largest possible territory at the net and thereby apply pressure on the receiver's return. Her second role is to poach the return, helping out the server by intercepting the crosscourt returns. The server's partner also needs the ability to fake—to simulate a movement as if she were going to poach—while remaining on her own side. The poaches and fakes create uncertainty in the mind of the receivers. Such uncertainty may in turn produce unforced errors on the return, either because the receiver will try a more difficult return or because he will feel rushed or distracted by the net player. The server's partner must make her presence felt at the net and approach each point with a mindset that says, "This ball is gonna be mine!"

This chapter answers questions frequently asked by the net player:

▮ *Is this my ball or not?* When the ball goes crosscourt more or less over the middle, the serving team is often confused about who is responsible for it. Pattern 13 outlines the territory of the server's partner at the net, to clarify which team member goes after a ball.

▌ *What do I do with the volley when the return is hit back to me?* Patterns 14 and 15 introduce the appropriate shot selection when volleying a return from a wide serve or a T serve.

▌ *What do I do if the return is crosscourt?* Patterns 16 and 17 present the movement patterns for the server's partner when the return is crosscourt and is played by the server.

▌ *Where do I go if the return is lobbed behind me?* Pattern 6 puts forward two options, depending on whether the server was serving and volleying or serving and staying back.

▌ *How can I become better at poaching?* Patterns 18 and 19 describe situations when the return is easy and the server's partner can poach per reaction, as well as situations in which she can anticipate the crosscourt return and poach per anticipation.

Note: We will present patterns for the poach per command or signal and the I formation in chapter 5 when we introduce patterns for the serving team as a unit, because the server's partner must plan these poaching actions with the server.

▌ Server's partner poaching on a crosscourt return.

Net territory of the server's partner

The server's partner's presence and coverage of territory at the net put pressure on the receiver. The more territory the server's partner is able to cover at the net, the greater the pressure he applies to the receiver's return.

Objective

To volley effectively any return hit inside the territory of the server's partner.

Challenge

To understand how positions at the net differ according to the type of serve and according to which territorial coverage by the server's partner most benefits the serving team.

Execution

In chapter 2 (page 23), we outlined the territory that the server's partner must cover on both a wide serve and a T serve. We demonstrated that regardless of serve location and the initial starting position of the server's partner, the limit of the territory the server's partner has to protect (T1 and T2) converges to the same point (TM) at three-quarters court. When drilling, therefore, the server's partner simply has to look behind himself to determine whether the ball passes inside or outside the marker at three-quarters court—indicating whether the return should have been played by him or by his partner (the server).

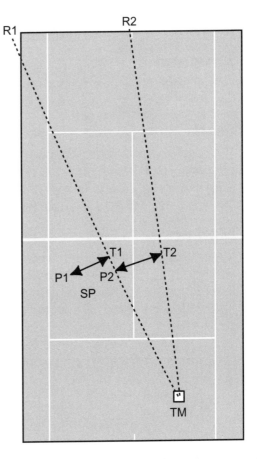

▌ Figure 4.1 illustrates the limits of the server's partner's territory, according to the following key:

Wide serve
R1—where contact is made on the return
P1—position where the server's partner moves to when the serve is wide
T1—limit of the territory at the net
TM—where the line representing the limit of the server's partner's territory (from R1 through T1) crosses three-quarters court

T serve
R2—where contact is made on the return
P2—position where the server's partner moves to when the serve is T
T2—limit of the territory at the net
TM—where the line representing the limit of the server's partner's territory (from R2 through T2) crosses three-quarters court

The distance from P1 to T1 and from P2 to T2 is the same, and the territorial limit for both serves is the same at three-quarters court (TM). Effective training of the server's partner's territory provides the server with a smaller space to cover.

13-1 BASKET FEED

Structure

Four players rotate as server's partner.
The coach feeds returns from his side of the court.

Feeds

The coach feeds returns from both wide serve (R1) and T serve (R2) returning positions. From R1, he aims the returns between line a (toward the doubles alley) and line b (toward the territory marker [TM]). From R2, he aims the returns between line c (toward the doubles alley) and line d (toward TM).

Markers

Marker P represents the starting position of the server's partner before the serve and (for this drill) before the coach moves to execute the feed returns in the R1 or R2 position. The server's partner waits in position P before moving to P1 for a wide serve return (R1) or to P2 for a T serve return (R2).

Targets

Volley away from the receiver and the receiver's partner.

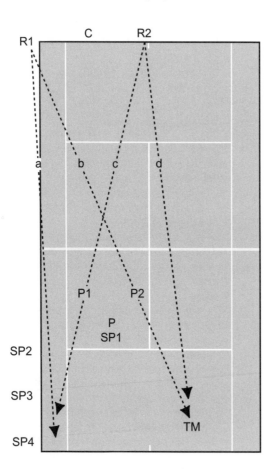

13-2 LIVE FEED

Structure

One server and one receiver.
Two net players rotate as the server's partner.

Feeds

The live feed requires one player to serve to a receiver.

Movement

The server calls out the serve location (wide or T) in advance so that his partner can move to P1 or P2 at the sound of the serve. This method also makes it easier for the receiver to move to the proper returning position (R1 or R2). The receiver challenges the server's partner's territory by hitting every return between the down-the-line alley and the territory marker at three-quarters court.

Server's Partner

If the server's partner does not touch a crosscourt return, he should look behind at the marker (TM) to see if the ball was inside his territory or not.

Markers

See drill 13-1.

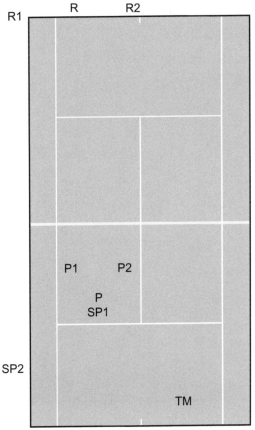

13-3 COOPERATIVE PLAY

Structure

Normal points are played, and the receiver challenges the net player right away with a return between the alley and the marker (TM) at three-quarters court. Note: If the return is too extremely crosscourt, then the server plays it. The server and server's partner agree on the serve location, either verbally or with a signal, so that the server's partner can move to P1 or P2 (previously learned) at the sound of the serve.

Server

Is ready to play the ball if it comes to him or to continue playing if his partner does not put the ball away.

Server's Partner

Tries to put the ball away.

Receiver

Places returns between the alley and marker (TM).

Receiver's Partner

Can play at either the service line or baseline.

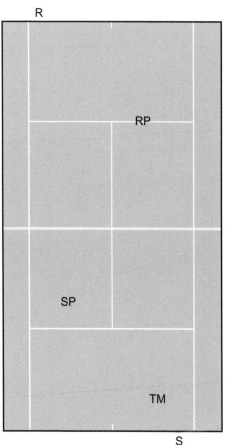

Volley down the middle after wide serve

As the server's partner becomes more proficient at covering her territory at the net, she will likely play more volleys and be increasingly challenged by the receiver's return. With very little time to make a decision regarding the volley, it is important for the server's partner to learn certain shot selection patterns so that they become automatic.

Objective

To develop the most common volley played by the server's partner after a wide serve—one that is directed between both players of the receiving team.

Challenge

Often when a receiver challenges the net player, she does it either through power returns requiring good reflexes or through a very accurate down-the-alley shot requiring quick movement.

Execution

As the receiver moves out of court to play the return, a space is created between the players of the receiving team. The server's partner must exploit this space.

14-1 LIVE FEED

Structure

Live feed drill.
One player serves wide.
One player returns between the down-the-line alley and the territory marker positioned at three-quarters court (TM).
Two players rotate in the role of server's partner and practice volleying toward the target in between their opponents. Move to P1 for wide serve, at the sound of the serve.

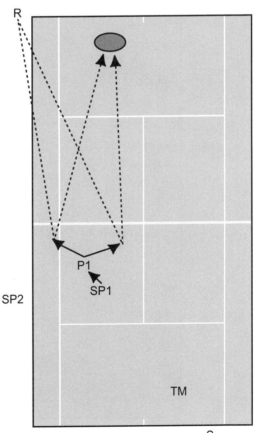

Angle volley after T serve

When serving T, especially on deuce side, the server's partner often receives a return in his territory as it is difficult for the receiver to do an inside out angle return that he rarely does in singles and which is technically challenging.

Objective

For the server's partner to learn to volley behind the receiver into the open court after a T serve.

Challenge

Whereas the forehand crosscourt volley on the deuce side represents a relatively easy volley, a backhand volley in the same direction (i.e., inside out) is particularly challenging and requires specific practice.

Execution

Remember to move close to the net at the sound of the serve, since the closer you are, the easier it is to angle the shot away from the receiver.

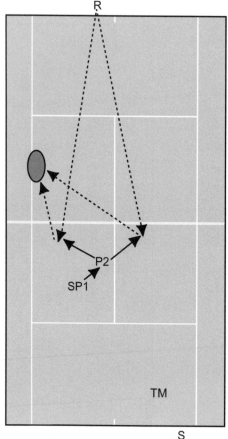

15-1 LIVE FEED

Structure

One player serves to the T.
One player returns between the alley and the marker positioned at three-quarters court (TM).
Two players rotate in the role of server's partner, practicing angled volleys toward the target and moving to P2 for T serve, at the sound of the serve.

Recovery to center after crosscourt return

Regardless of how good the net player is, he will not be able to intercept every ball. The receiver will succeed in returning many good crosscourt returns back to the server.

Objective

As soon as the server's partner realizes that he cannot volley the ball, he needs to adjust his position quickly at the net by recovering toward the center of the court.

Execution

The server's partner needs to move toward the middle and slightly backwards. He does so in order to be in a good position if the server volleys down the line to the receiver's partner. If the server plays the volley crosscourt, however, he must move toward the alley so that he and the server are in a strong position at the net (see pattern 24, pages 129-130).

16-1 COOPERATIVE POINT ON DOWN-THE-LINE FIRST VOLLEY

Structure

Basket feed and playing out the point.
The coach (as receiver) introduces a crosscourt return of serve (line 1) and the players play out the point.
Two players (S1, S2) rotate to simulate a serve-and-volley play.
One player as the server's partner (SP).
One player as the receiver's partner (RP).

Server

Volleys down the line (line 2) to challenge the reciever's partner.

Server's Partner

Moves back quickly to the center of the court and is ready to reflex the volley back from the receiver's partner.

Receiver's Partner

Volleys crosscourt (line 3), challenging the server's partner.

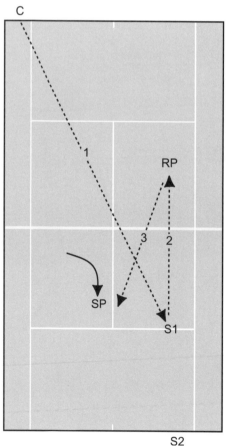

16-2 COOPERATIVE POINT ON CROSSCOURT FIRST VOLLEY

Structure

Basket feed and playing out the point.
The coach (as receiver) introduces a crosscourt return of serve (line a), and players play out the point after the second shot.
Two players (S1, S2) rotate to simulate serve-and-volley.

Server

Simulates serve-and-volley by moving in (line 1); volleys crosscourt (line b) and quickly recovers toward the middle (line 2).

Server's Partner

Quickly moves toward the middle as the feed goes crosscourt to the server (line 1), and then moves toward the alley (line 2) when server volleys crosscourt.

Coach (as receiver)

When the coach plays back the server's crosscourt volley, he will regularly challenge the server's partner's recovery with shots played down the line.

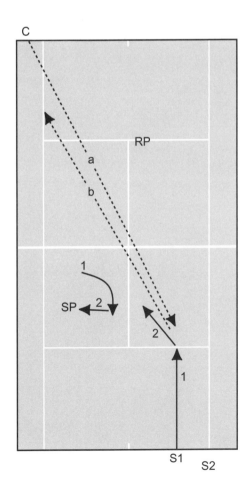

Movement patterns when server stays back

This pattern applies when the return is crosscourt and goes back to the server, who has chosen to stay back.

Objective

The server's partner must move back to the service line and toward the middle in order to better cover the court and ready herself in the event that the server's second shot is intercepted by the net player. The server's partner then determines where to move next, depending on the quality of the server's crosscourt shot:

- Offensive shot—gets close to the net and reinforces the middle to intercept the next shot.

- Neutral or defensive shot—moves slightly toward the alley to cover a potential down-the-line passing shot attempt.

Challenge

If the server's partner does not back up, she may be a target for a put-away volley by the receiver's partner. If she does not move forward at the appropriate time, she may miss an opportunity to intercept the ball.

17-1 COOPERATIVE POINT ON CROSSCOURT RALLY FROM BASELINE

Structure

Basket feed; normal points are played.
The coach (as receiver) introduces a crosscourt return of serve and the players play out the point.
Two players rotate as the server's partner, practicing the movement.

Server

Completes the point crosscourt with the coach and looks to drive the ball to set up his partner at the net.

Server's Partner

Moves to M1 on a neutral shot, protecting against down-the-line passing attempts, or to M2 on an offensive shot, attempting to intercept the next shot.

Receiver's Partner

Does not poach as he knows that the server will play crosscourt to train the server's partner's movement.

Receiver

The coach plays out the point. When receiving easy balls, he challenges the server's partner with down-the-line shots. He also provides some easy balls for the server to drive crosscourt and set up his partner.

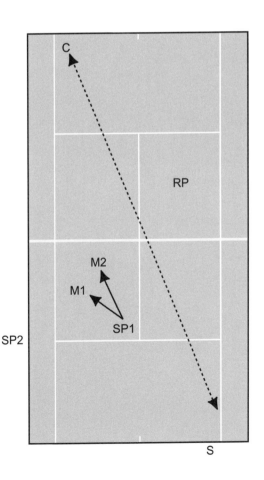

Movement patterns after a lob return

The server's partner needs to master different movement patterns when being lobbed by the receiver, as he or the server can retrieve the lob.

Objective

Server's partner practices movement and shot selection patterns when smashing or retrieving the lob and when the server retrieves the lob.

Challenge and Execution

The lob is often the tactic that creates many problems for the serving team, as they often feel unorganized and don't know where to position themselves. It is important for the server's partner to train the basic movement and shot selection patterns according to these five tactical situations:

- Server's partner smashes: drill 18-1
- Server's partner retrieves a lob landing behind him: drill 18-2
- Server crosses and smashes the lob: drill 18-3
- Server moves in and retrieves the lob: drill 18-4
- Server stays back and retrieves the lob: drill 18-5

18-1 SERVER'S PARTNER SMASHES

Structure

Basket feed; normal points are played.
The coach introduces the lob and the point begins with the server's partner smashing.

Server

The server simulates a serve-and-volley in order to be at the net to play out the point if the smash is returned defensively.

Receiver and Receiver's Partner

Move back to adopt a more defensive position against the smash.

Server's Partner

After smashing, recovers toward the net to maintain the attack.

Coach

After introducing the lob, the coach backs up and ensures that each player follows his assigned role while playing the point.

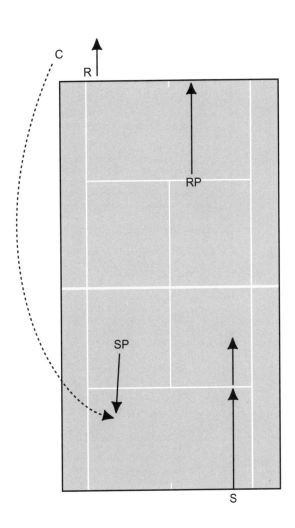

18-2 SERVER'S PARTNER RETRIEVES THE LOB

Structure

Basket feed; normal points are played.
The coach introduces the lob. The server simulates a serve-and-volley; the server's partner lets the lob land behind him and chases it down.

Server

Joins his partner at the baseline to defend if he lobs.

Receiver

Moves in when he sees the lob landing behind the net player.

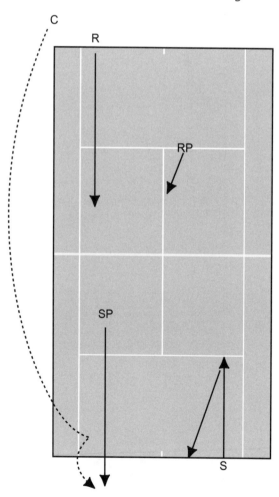

Server's Partner

Mixes up lobs and drives and recovers accordingly.

Receiver's Partner

Moves forward to be ready for a crosscourt lob or a drive.

Coach

After introducing the lob, the coach backs up and ensures that each player follows his assigned role while playing the point.

18-3 SERVER CROSSES AND SMASHES

Structure

Basket feed; normal points are played.
The coach introduces the lob. The server's partner lets the lob go behind him; the server simulates a serve-and-volley and switches sides to execute a backhand smash.

Server

Simulates a serve-and-volley before the coach feeds the lob. The server recovers forward after the smash to maintain the attack.

Receiver and Receiver's Partner

Move back to defend against the smash.

Server's Partner

Switches sides, toward the service line, and seeks to maintain the attack at the net.

Coach

After introducing the lob, the coach backs up and ensures that each player follows his assigned role while playing the point.

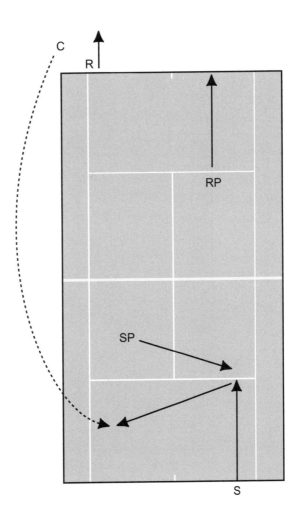

18-4 SERVER MOVES IN AND RETRIEVES THE LOB

Structure

Basket feed; normal points are played.

The coach introduces the lob. The server's partner lets the lob land behind him; the server simulates a serve-and-volley and switches sides to retrieve the lob after the bounce.

Server

Lobs—mixes drives when possible.

Server's Partner

Switches sides and moves quickly to the baseline in the event that the server lobs.

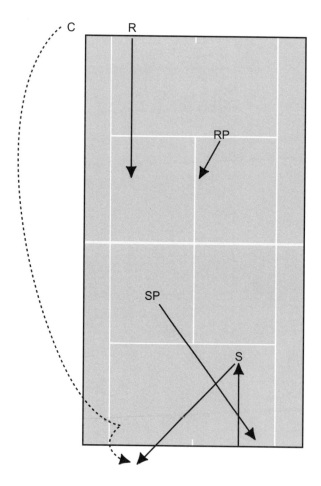

Receiver and Receiver's Partner

Move in to attack.

Coach

After introducing the lob, the coach backs up and ensures that each player follows his assigned role while playing the point.

18-5 SERVER STAYS BACK AND RETRIEVES THE LOB

Structure

Basket feed; normal points are played.
The coach introduces the lob. The server's partner lets the lob land behind him; the server stays back after the serve, having only to change sides to handle the lob.

Server

Has time to set up and mixes up drives, angles, or offensive lobs.

Server's Partner

Switches sides and stays at the service line, because the server can provide a quality shot.

Receiver and Receiver's Partner

Move forward to attack.

Coach

After introducing the lob, the coach backs up and ensures that each player follows his assigned role while playing the point.

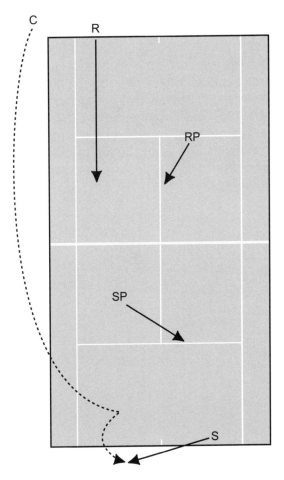

Poaching per reaction

This situation arises when the receiver returns a defensive shot or normal cross-court rallying shot with a slightly high trajectory that passes over the middle of the court.

Objective

The server's partner must learn to leave her territory to poach per reaction.

Challenge

The server's partner must have a "this ball is mine" attitude and act accordingly. This mind-set requires discipline, because an opportunity to poach per reaction may arise only a few times each match. When performed, it sends a clear message to the opponent that she cannot expect to defend safely.

Execution

If the server's partner contacts the volley quite high, she should hit it toward the receiver's partner at midcourt. If she contacts the volley lower, she should angle it back to the receiver's side. The server should not expect her partner's volley to end the point, and should change sides immediately.

Drills

The key with drilling is to provide sufficient repetition that the players have ample opportunity to develop the aggressive mind-set and the assertive decision-making abilities that are such an essential feature of the poach per reaction. Drilling with basket feeds can be used to develop this skill before players feel comfortable incorporating it into game situations. To develop real reaction habits, the feeds should be mixed up to provide situations in which the crosscourt return cannot be poached and some in which it can be poached per reaction.

19-1 BASKET FEED

Structure

Basket feed; normal points are played.
The coach (as receiver) feeds a return to initiate the point.
Two players rotate at net to practice the poach per reaction.
Two players take the roles of server and receiver's partner to play out the point.
The coach ensures proper competitive attitude and he checks to see the decision-making is done quickly.

Feeds

The coach introduces four feeds from a wide serve position to train the players' decision-making abilities and shot selection when they play as the server's partner. These feeds are the following:

1. Down the line, to challenge the player's territory (line a)

2. Hard crosscourt, which is too difficult to poach per reaction (line b)

3. Angled crosscourt, which is too far away from the player to poach per reaction (line c)

4. Defensive floater (for intermediate levels) or a normal rallying shot (for advanced levels), which the player should poach per reaction (line d)

Server's Partner

Moves to P1 just before coach feeds from wide serve position to protect his territory, and also moves when he sees a defensive floater (see pattern 13, pages 95-98).
When poaching the movement needs to be diagonal toward the net to be as close as possible to put the shot away.

Markers

A marker at three-quarters court (TM) identifies the territory that the server's partner must protect.

Targets

The server's partner uses these guidelines to aid her shot selection:

1. Play to the receiver's partner (RP) when poaching a high return.

2. Play an angled volley when the return is lower.

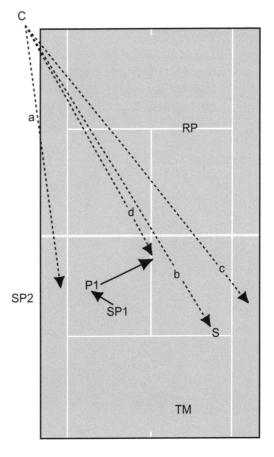

Poaching per anticipation

There are two types of anticipation (see chapter 2 on poaching per anticipation, pages 24-26):

• Technical anticipation is determined by a particular way of hitting the ball.

• Tactical anticipation relates to the tendencies of the opponent or his specific shot selection. For example, when using a slice return most players will play an angled crosscourt return and mix this up with some lobs.

Objective

To develop skills of observation and therefore of tactical and technical anticipation.

Challenge

To anticipate and time the poach correctly (i.e., not to move too early). Poaching per anticipation is the most difficult poach to master. With poaching per reaction you are sure that the ball is crosscourt, and with poaching per command you know that the server will change sides as you poach. Neither of these certainties applies with anticipation—hence its difficulty.

Execution

The coach should encourage players to access their anticipatory abilities while they play the points. He should emphasize that whereas a poach per anticipation may not always result in the team winning the point, it will (if performed well) put increasing pressure on the receiving team over the course of a match.

20-1 COOPERATIVE POINT

Structure

The cooperative point drill provides the volume necessary for developing the skill of poaching on a good return, simulating a situation in which the server's partner anticipated well.

Server

Serves and changes sides only when the server's partner is doing the volley, as would happen in a match, even though he knows beforehand that there will be a poach.

Receiver

Plays solid crosscourt returns even though he knows that the server's partner is going to poach.

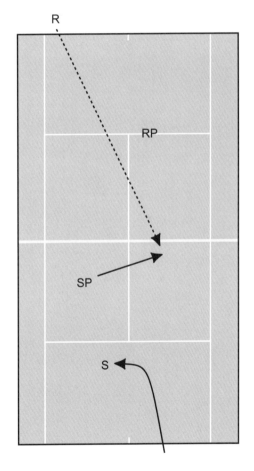

Server's Partner

Plays out the point competitively, using these shot selections:

1. Play to the receiver's partner when poaching a high return.

2. Play an angled crosscourt volley when the return is lower.

Receiver's Partner

May choose to play back if he prefers to defend with his groundstrokes than with his volleys.

Drill Variation

Play normal points where the server's partner will poach per anticipation when he feels technically or tactically, that the receiver will play crosscourt. If the server's partner moves to poach, but is passed down the line by the receiver, ask the receiver if it was intentional (therefore, wrong anticipation) if he saw the server's partner moving too early (and changed his shot). This enables the server's partner to verify his anticipation and timing for changing sides.

5

SERVING TEAM PATTERNS AND DRILLS

Great doubles teams use team tactics in an attempt to dictate the point from the outset, as well as to put pressure on the receiving team. By using such tactics, they not only develop a basic game style but also have the tools to counter great crosscourt returns or pressure exerted by the forward movement of the receiver's partner.

This chapter will address systematically three frequent questions related to team play when serving:

▌ How do we train the specific tactics to initiate the points (poaching per command or signal, the Australian formation, and the I formation)?

▌ How do we protect the court when we are both at the net? How far from the net should we be? Who takes the middle?

▌ Where should we volley to finish the point?

Patterns 21 through 23 outline the poaching per command or signal and special formations like the Australian and I formations. The serving team agrees on all these tactics before the point starts. Refer to chapter 2

❚ Serving teams are using special formations, like this I formation used by Jonas Bjorkman and Todd Woodbridge, to create more pressure on the receiving teams.

for detailed discussion of these movements and formations, since we will present only the playing situation drill here.

Patterns 24 through 28 explain what territory each member of the serving team needs to cover when both are at the net and how to move most effectively as a team in this situation. It is of utmost importance to know exactly where one's partner is positioned laterally and to feel both at the same distance to the net. Such awareness provides the confidence and teamwork that helps each partner to know who is taking which ball.

Patterns 29 through 31 describe the best volley options to use at the net when playing against different receiving team formations.

Remember to train on both the deuce and ad sides of the court for all drills.

Court coverage when poaching per command

Objective

We have more control over the frequency of poaching when we command it rather than simply waiting for the server's partner to poach per reaction or anticipation. Such a tactic is also more effective in the event that the receiver chooses to hit down the line, because the server will be able to cover the return, having changed sides.

Poaching per command is a must when a team is losing too many points because of the following:

- The quality of the crosscourt returns, especially those that are angled. The poacher intercepts the crosscourt returns and forces the receiver to execute down-the-line returns sometimes, since the receiver does not know when a poach will occur.

- The receiver's partner moving forward and placing too much pressure on the server's first volley or groundstroke. Poaching actions make the receiver's partner hesitate when closing in, because she could get hit by a poach if she is too close to the net.

Challenge

The real challenge of poaching lies in understanding where to move in order to cover the court as a team. When a serving team uses this tactic regularly, the receiver will likely return a greater number of balls down the line. The server's partner must therefore be aware of this possibility and adapt her movement accordingly.

Execution

In order to disguise the poaching, it is important that both players move initially forward before changing sides.

Drills

A progression of three cooperative points is needed to prepare players to perform the poach per command well.

21-1 POACHING PER COMMAND ON A WIDE SERVE

Structure

The figure shows the basic positions and movements used when poaching per command on a wide serve. A sequence of four drills provides a progression in practicing this specific skill. Players play cooperative points in both closed and open game situation drills.

1. Closed game situation drill for the server's partner

The receiver always returns crosscourt between A and B. The crosscourt return allows the server's partner to practice the poaching movement to the middle of the court facing the net and the put-away volley from either the forehand or backhand.

2. Closed game situation drill for the server

The receiver always returns down the line between the alley and A, to allow the server to practice moving across and volleying down the line back to the receiver.

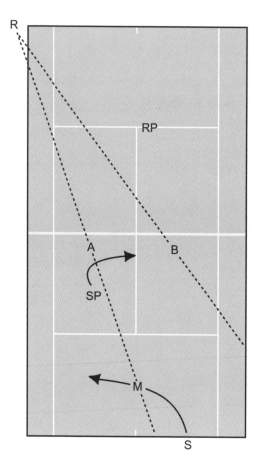

3. Open game situation drill for the serving team

The receiver returns crosscourt or down the line, to allow the serving team to practice with some uncertainty about which player will take the volley. The coach observes whether they disguise the movement.

4. Game situation with a wide serve

Real points are played with or without poaching. Thus the serving team can both discover whether they have mastered the poaching action and determine its impact on the receiving team.

The figure clearly demonstrates that the server's partner does not need to cross the middle line to cover his territory (represented as the area between A and B). A flat marker (M) divides the territory between the server and her partner, showing who should have taken the ball if it passed between them.

21-2 POACHING PER COMMAND ON A T SERVE

Structure

The figure shows the basic positions and movements used when poaching per command on a T serve. A sequence of four drills (playing cooperative points—closed and open game situations) provides a progression in practicing this specific skill.

1. Closed game situation drill for the server's partner

The receiver always returns inside out between A and B. The crosscourt return allows the server's partner to practice the poaching movement to the middle of the court facing the net and the put-away volley from either the forehand or backhand.

2. Closed game situation drill for the server

The receiver always returns down the line between the alley and A, to allow the server to practice moving across and volleying down the line back to the receiver.

3. Open game situation drill for the serving team

The receiver returns inside out or down the line, to allow the serving team to practice with some uncertainty about which player will take the volley. The coach observes whether they disguise the movement.

4. Game situation with a T serve

Real points are played with or without poaching. Thus the serving team can both discover whether they have mastered the poaching action and determine its impact on the receiving team.

The net player needs to cross the middle line to cover the crosscourt return on a T serve. Lines A and B show the server's partner's territory for the poach.

A flat marker (M) divides the territory between the server and her partner, showing who should have taken the ball if it passed between them.

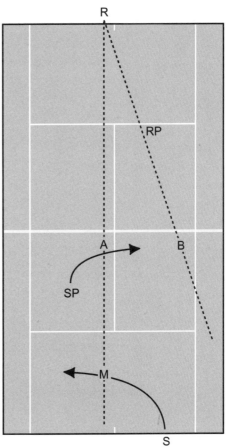

21-3 NORMAL POINTS PLAYED WITH OR WITHOUT POACHING

Structure

Normal points are played.

Serving Team

Talks before every point to determine the serve location and whether they will poach (see figure for basic positioning). The team should also experiment with hand signals to become familiar with this mode of communication (see figure 2.10, page 28).

Comments

On a second serve it may be decided in advance that the poach is canceled.

Receiving Team

No constraints.

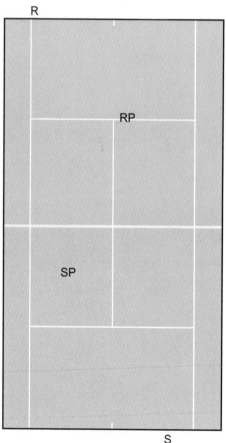

Coach

Provides feedback on how the serving team implemented the poach. She also introduces the notion of faking a poach at the net to distract the receiver. After the practice, the coach discusses with the serving and receiving teams their experiences in these game situations.

The Australian formation

The Australian formation is characterized by the server's partner being on the same side as the server. It is predominantly performed on the ad side.

Objective

To remove the receiver's crosscourt return and force the return to be played down the line. The serving team more commonly uses it on the ad side, because most receivers experience greater difficulty returning down the line with the backhand than with the forehand. Also, if a server stays back, performing the Australian formation to the ad side allows the server to change sides and play the return with his forehand rather than his backhand—an option that appeals to most players.

The Australian formation is also used when the receiver's partner is moving forward and applying considerable pressure to the second shot of the server (volley or groundstroke). In these situations, it allows the server to play back down the line to the receiver without having the receiver's partner in front of him.

Challenge

The server has to be quick about getting into position to cover the probable down-the-line return. For this reason, the I formation, which creates more uncertainty for the receiver about where to return, has replaced the Australian formation at the professional level. The Australian formation is still very effective at the club level, especially on the ad side, because the receivers have more difficulty returning their backhand down the line, and it allows the server, who is staying back, to change sides to their forehand.

Execution

With the Australian, the intention is clear that the serving team wants to remove the crosscourt return. Therefore, the server should change sides immediately after the serve.

Drills

This pattern can be trained effectively through structured point play.

22-1 COOPERATIVE POINT

Structure

Normal points are played, with the serving team adopting the Australian formation.

Server

Changes sides quickly and tries to hit his second shot down the line back to the receiver.

Receiver

Has no constraints, but focuses on being consistent and tries not to hit winners down the line, since this drill is set up to help the serving team practice the use of the Australian formation.

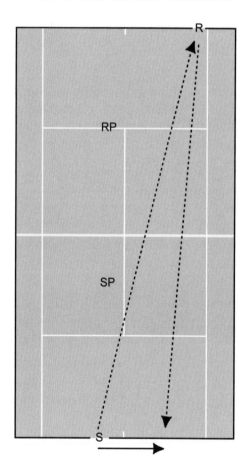

Coach

Encourages the serving team to be attentive to this formation's effect: Was the receiver bothered by having to attempt a down-the-line return? Was it easier to set up a first volley or forehand drive (without the receiver's partner in front to intercept the cross-court shot)?

The I formation

This tactic is called the I formation because the serving team is almost in a straight line. That is, the server is positioned close to the middle in preparation to serve, and her partner is crouching or kneeling down on the middle line, ready to move to either the right or the left according to their verbal or signaled agreement.

Objective

Serving teams use this formation for several reasons:

- To form part of a game style that involves moving and poaching a lot
- To place pressure on the receiver through uncertainty about the net player's movements
- To remove the crosscourt return by poaching 70 percent of the time from this position
- To remove the pressure that the receiver's partner imposes when moving forward to intercept the server's first volley

Challenge

To understand that the server's partner can assume four different positions after the serve, depending on whether it is a wide or a T serve and on whether a poach is performed. Refer to chapter 2 (page 36) for a detailed explanation of this concept.

Execution

Server's partner

- There are variations possible for the server's partner. He could kneel or crouch down. He can be closer of further away from the net. He can position himself on the middle line or beside it.
- At the sound of the serve, he moves forward to disguise the movement and then quickly takes his usual position when the team is either poaching per command (pattern 20, pages 114-115) or not poaching (pattern 13, pages 95-98).

Drills

Cooperative closed playing situations to cooperative open playing situations.

23-1 I FORMATION WITHOUT POACHING

1. Closed game situation drill for the server's partner

The receiver returns either forehand or backhand down the line. For the server's partner to practice her movement and net play, she should move forward slightly at the sound of the serve (so that the receiver does not know whether she will poach) before assuming position M1 for serves aimed wide (R1) and M2 for T serves (R2). The figure below illustrates these movements and positions.

2. Closed game situation drill for the server

The receiver returns crosscourt using forehand or backhand. The crosscourt return allows the server to practice moving into position and hitting her second shot (volley or groundstroke) crosscourt as usual to the receiver.

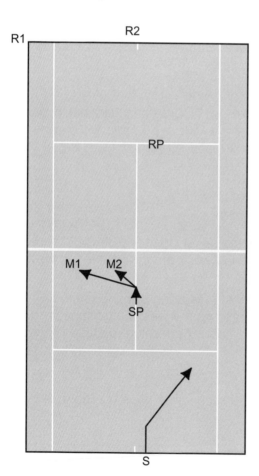

3. Open game situation drill for the serving team

The receiver returns crosscourt or down the line. Varying the returns allows the serving team to practice their movements with an element of uncertainty, since they do not know who will receive the return—the server (crosscourt return) or the server's partner (down-the-line return). The receiver should mix up the returns even if she knows the movements of the serving team.

23-2 I FORMATION WITH POACHING

1. Closed game situation drill for the server's partner

The receiver returns crosscourt with either forehand or backhand. For the server's partner to practice her movement and net play, she should move forward slightly at the sound of the serve (so that the receiver cannot anticipate the movement) before assuming position M3 for a wide serve (R1) or M4 for a T serve (R2). The figure below shows these positions.

2. Closed game situation drill for the server

The receiver hits down-the-line forehand and backhand returns. These returns allow the server to practice moving into position and hitting her second shot (volley or groundstroke) down the line back to the receiver.

3. Open game situation drill for the serving team

The receiver returns crosscourt or down the line. This variety allows the serving team to practice their movements with an element of uncertainty, since they do not know who will receive the return. The receiver should mix up the returns even if she knows the movements of the serving team.

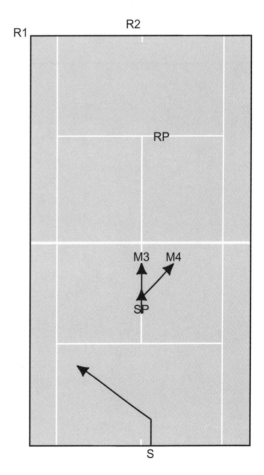

23-3 I FORMATION WITH OR WITHOUT POACHING

Structure

Normal points are played.

Serving Team

Talks between points to determine serve location and whether they will poach (see figure below for basic positioning on this drill). They can also experiment with the use of signals, especially on the second serve, to become familiar with this mode of communication. On a second serve the team may assume a normal position instead of the I formation.

Receiving Team

No constraints.

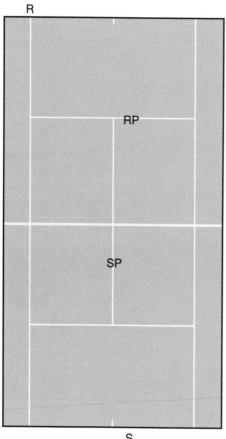

Coach

Provides feedback on the implementation of team formation and movements and emphasizes the importance of disguising the poach by moving forward before taking their respective positioning. Also discusses with the serving and receiving teams their experiences in these game situations.

Lateral positioning when both players at the net

The serving team is at the net as the receiver prepares to play his second shot from the alley.

Objective

To cover the court according to the angles of the two best (most extreme) down-the-line and angled shots of the opponent. Positioning for such coverage places the crosscourt player (the server) at the net standing on the middle line.

Challenge

To cover the court as a team, rather than having each player concerned only with covering his side of the court. Mentally it can be difficult for the server to position himself in the middle of the court, since he may feel he is leaving his court open.

Drill

The basket feed drill explains the rationale of proper positioning.

24-1 BASKET FEED

Before the drill, the coach explains the lateral positioning. He extends a rope from the receiver's corner to the other side of the court so that it replicates the trajectory of an angled shot (M1). He then explains that this boundary and the sideline (M2), which represents the down-the-line shot, help determine the territory the serving team needs to cover. The coach identifies the middle of this territory (M3) and extends another rope along the midline, dividing the space in half, so that the serving partners can appreciate who should cover what.

Structure

Two teams of two players rotate at the net positions.

Feeds

The coach feeds balls from the corner, where the receiver would be after an approach shot by the server. He mixes up all shots, with a focus on challenging the area between the two players (M3).

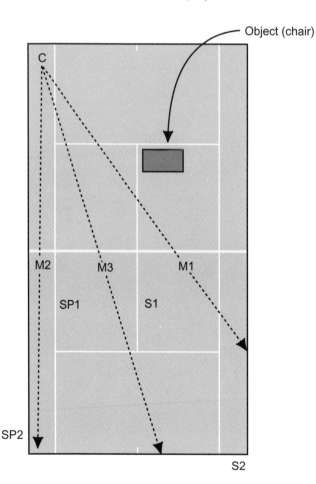

Object (chair)

Movement

By observing the angles in the figure, it becomes clear that the crosscourt player handles any ball that goes directly over the middle and even some balls on his partner's side of the court. This crosscourt player is the server who, having played a first volley, recovers to the middle and covers the crosscourt drives, the lobs, and the angled shots.

Markers

As stated in coach's explanation.

Target

The serving team tries to direct the volley away from the receiver and from the target representing the receiver's partner (e.g., a chair).

Lateral court movements when both players at the net

This situation occurs when both players on the receiving team are at the baseline and the serving team is at the net.

Objective

The best type of lateral movement is the so-called *windshield wiper*. Players move together as if attached by a rope, to the right or to the left, according to which member of the receiving team will hit the shot.

Challenge

Each net player must take her proper position when moving side to side, before the opponent hits the ball.

25-1 LIVE FEED—"WINDSHIELD WIPERS"

Structure

A rally situation with two players on the serving side at the net and two players on the receiving side at the baseline.

Movement

When the ball goes to receiver 1, the net players move to their position (1). When it goes to receiver's partner (2), they assume position (2). This movement from left to right and right to left resembles the movement of a windshield wiper.

Coach

From behind the serving team, the coach observes and encourages quick positioning before the baseliners hit the ball.

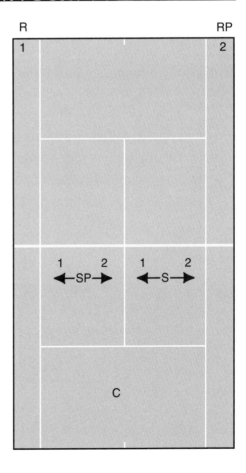

Correct distance from net when both players at the net

Objective

To determine the appropriate distance players should position themselves from the net.

Challenge

Players' distance from the net depends on their ability to cover the lob. Obviously the professionals can play much closer to the net than intermediate players, because of their greater athletic capabilities and therefore effectiveness in retreating backwards to cover the lob with a smash.

Execution

Players should generally aim to stand around the middle of the service box. From this position, players can quickly make two steps forward to be very close to the net to put away an easy ball, or move three steps back to cross the service line and cover a deep lob.

Drills

To master this pattern, players need to develop the decision-making ability to determine when to move forward and when to move backward. From the net position, players need to practice the following:

- Staying put (performing what is called *the wall*) to deal with strong drives
- Moving forward to easy balls or angled shots to finish the point
- Backing up quickly to execute a smash

26-1 CLOSED DRILL WITH BOTH PLAYERS AT THE NET

Structure

Basket feed drill.

Two teams of two players rotate at the net.

The coach explains the setup for this closed drill. Flat markers in the service boxes indicate the forward and backward limits between which players can position themselves anywhere they choose.

Feeds

Coach feeds, in a known sequence, three different common shots hit from the corner—drive, dink, and lob.

Movement

Players respond to each shot as follows:

1. Drive—Players do the wall (see pattern 28).

2. Dink—Players move in to the net.

3. Lob—Players move to cross the service line before the lob.

Markers

Place markers indicating the forward limit (dotted line 1)—too close to the net will leave them vulnerable to a lob. Place markers indicating the backward limit (dotted line 2)—too far from the net will make it difficult to put the volley away easily.

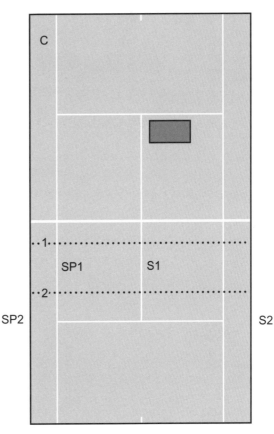

Covering the lob when both players at the net

When being lobbed two questions need to be answered:

1. Who should take the smash?

When the serving team is at the net, each player tries to take his own smash since there is no one behind to cover it. If the lob is between them, the ad court player (when there are two right-handed players) asks for it. If the lob is between a lefty and a righty, communication is important and the first one to call for the smash is the one who takes it.

2. Who should chase down the lob?

Both players should make a move for the lob in case one of them is surprised or wrong-footed and is therefore late to chase it. In general, the first player who crosses the service line should indicate that he will retrieve the lob. Because a return lob is highly probable if your partner is in trouble when chasing down an opponent's lob, both players should end up at the baseline in order to defend against the smash.

27-1 FIRST PLAYER TO CROSS THE SERVICE LINE TAKES THE LOB

Structure

Basket feed drills.
Two players as servers rotating at the net.
Two players as server's partner rotating at the net.
Coach as the receiver simulating a lob or drive groundstroke.

Objective

The server and server's partner will be trained to cover all lobs. In most situations, the player who has the quickest reaction to the lob, will cross the service line first and call "mine" immediately.

Note: Only the first drill will be illustrated.

1st drill: training the server to cover every lob (see diagram)

Server covers

- Lob down the line (line a)
- Lob crosscourt (line b)
- Drive crosscourt (line c)

Server's partner is instructed not to react to the lob, but will move back to the baseline when his partner is retrieving it.

2nd drill: training the server's partner to cover every lob

Server is instructed not to react to the lob, but will move back to the baseline when his partner is retrieving it.

Server's partner will have to cover

- Lob down the line
- Lob crosscourt
- Drive down the line

3rd drill: training the serving team to effectively cover the lobs

Coach mixes up the feeds and when there is a lob, each player tries to smash it. If unable to do so, the first one to cross the service line will call "mine" and take the lob.

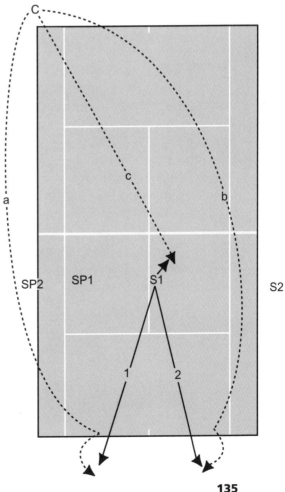

The wall

The wall refers to both players of the serving team choosing to stay in their positions to volley back their opponents' drives. As the point progresses and every ball hit by their opponents is returned back by the volleys of the serving team, the action bears a resemblance to two players hitting against a wall. This situation is particularly common when the opponent hits too hard for the serving players to be comfortable in moving forward, very close to the net, to volley a winner.

Objective

• Against both players at the baseline—This situation is common when the receiving team stays back in order to challenge the net players with their big groundstrokes. The serving team as the net players, remain steady until a weaker shot or a lob is provided for them to move forward to put away the volley or to move backward and smash.

• Against a one up–one back formation—The serving team plays every volley back to the receiver at the baseline until she either misses or provides the serving team an easier ball from which they can finish the point. If the receiver's partner has weak volleys, the serving team may immediately redirect the receiver's shot toward the receiver's partner to pressure her.

Execution

• In order to force an easier ball earlier, the net players try to volley to the weaker opponent or to the weakest counterattacking stroke of the receiving team.

• The lateral movement seen in pattern 25 (the windshield wiper) is important when using the wall against two players at the back.

Note: When training the wall, coaches need to remember to mix up the feeds in order to develop the serving team's mind-set of moving from the neutral position—either forward to an easy ball or backward to a lob.

• The distance at which the players will play the wall is anywhere between the lines of markers A and B (see diagram on page 137). In front of line A is too close to the net and vulnerable to a lob. Behind line B is too far from the net to put volleys away easily.

28-1 THE WALL AGAINST BOTH BACK

Structure

Cooperative play.
Serving team is at the net.
Receiving team is at the baseline.

Serving Team

The server feeds an easy ball, simulating an approach volley. After the receiver's drive groundstroke, the serving team continues using the wall tactics against the drive—in other words, by remaining between the lines of flat markers A and B while looking to move forward on easier shots.

Receiving Team

After the server's feed, the receiver starts the point with a drive. Both players try to maintain powerful drives with their groundstrokes throughout the point.

Coach

The coach provides feedback on the decisions made by the serving team in performing the wall and moving forward or backward when required.

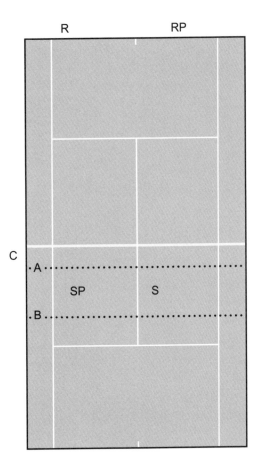

Shot selection against one up and one back

Objective

To develop the skills to play the most appropriate volley or smash according to the type of shot received at the net.

Challenge

To make quick decisions on shot selection in order to volley effectively.

Execution

When able to play a punch volley or smash, players at the net aim at the closest opponent because he will have less time to defend effectively.

When receiving balls that are lower or more difficult to play, players will play either

- a defensive shot back to the baseline player, or
- an offensive shot, like an angled or drop volley, to the player positioned at the baseline.

29-1 SERVING TEAM AGAINST ONE UP AND ONE BACK

Structure

Basket feed points.
Serving team is at the net.
Receiver is at the baseline and receiver's partner is at the service line.
Coach feeds the ball from the receiver's corner and then leaves the court to let the receiver play out the point.

Feeds

Coach mixes up easy down-the-line lobs (line a), down-the-middle drives (line b), and slower shots (line c).

Serving team

Serving team chooses from these movements and basic shot selections:

- Against the lob, quick movement back and smash at the receiver's partner (line 1)
- Against the drive, doing the wall back to the receiver (line 2)
- Against the slower ball, quick movement toward the net and doing an angle or drop volley (line 3)

Receiving Team

As soon as the ball is sent, the receiving team will compete normal points.

Coach

Besides providing feeds, the coach gives feedback on shot selection and encourages players to maintain the positioning and movement as seen in the previous drill (28-1).

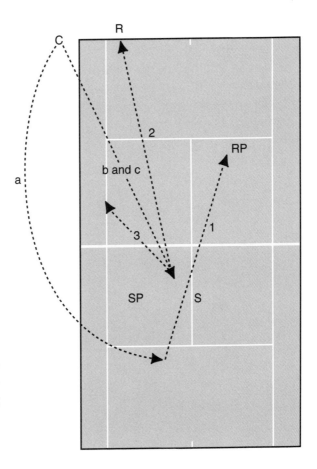

Shot selection against both back

Having the receiving team at the baseline is common on clay courts as well as when a receiving team is playing defensively against a serving team that poaches or often uses the I formation.

Objective

To teach players how to choose appropriate shots for winning points when both receivers are at the baseline.

Challenge

In this situation, it is difficult to win the point as quickly as would otherwise be the case. Players should use the wall if there are drives and try to volley back to the weaker player, who should be the first to either miss or provide an easier ball so that the serving team can put the volley away.

Execution

To create openings, the serving team at the net can select from four shots:

1. Play to the weakest player.

2. Hit down the middle to open up the court to the side of the player who will hit the ball.

3. Hit an angle to remove the player from her baseline position and then volley between the two players.

4. Hit a drop shot and either play to the open court or hit back to the player who chased the drop shot.

30-1 SERVING TEAM AT NET AGAINST TWO PLAYERS AT BASELINE

Structure

Cooperative points.
Serving team is at the net.
Receiving team is at the baseline.

Serving Team

After feeding a ball to either baseliner, the point starts with the serving team looking to implement the following shot selection:

- Line 1—down the middle
- Line 2—angle
- Line 3—drop shot

Receiving Team

Play normal points.

Coach

Helps players to identify their best shots and raises their awareness about the potential weaknesses of the other team. For example, lines of volleys 2 and 3 will challenge the receiver's court coverage, and the line of volley 1 will challenge the quality of their strokes.

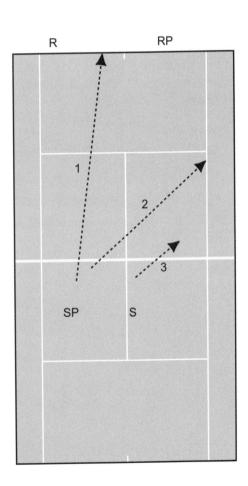

Shot selection against both at net

Having both receivers at the net is not particularly common but can occur with increasing regularity when two experienced doubles teams meet each other.

Objective

Tactically, the old truth about playing to the weakness prevails, since there is often one player who volleys less effectively than the other. The serving team therefore seeks to isolate this player, looking for a mistake or an easier ball to put away.

Alternatively, depending on their level of confidence, the serving team may also try to simply outrally the opponents. However, this option is not as effective as trying to set up the point with an angled volley, which achieves both objectives:

- It provides a volley up that can be attacked.
- It opens up the court to volley in between the receiving team.

Challenge

In this situation, players know that they need to keep the ball low, since any floater will signal the end of the point and potentially be physically dangerous for them.

Execution

Once again, the serving team focuses on shot selection:

- Isolate the player with the weaker volleys.
- Outrally the opponents in a duel of quick volleys.
- Set up a put-away volley with an angled volley.

DRILL 31-1 BASKET DRILL—ISOLATE ONE PLAYER

Structure

Cooperative points.
Two servers against two receivers, both teams playing at the net.

Feeds

The coach feeds the server a low volley and asks the serving team to play out the point.

Serving Team

The serving team tries to isolate the deuce or ad side player to get used to playing to the weaker player.

Receiving Team

Plays normal points.

Coach

The coach provides feedback on players' shot selection and tactics.

Note: When the serving team receives an easy shot from the player they isolate, they can volley anywhere, but should consider to finish the point against the stronger player for psychological value.

DRILL 31-2 BASKET DRILL—ANGLED VOLLEY TO SET UP PUT-AWAY VOLLEY

Structure

Two servers against two receivers, both teams playing at the net.

Feeds

The coach feeds the server a low volley and asks him to angle the volley.

Serving Team

Will close down the net after the angled volley until proven that the opponent can execute a successful lob volley. If the lob volley can happen, they will remain halfway between the net and the service line to cover the lob and then be ready to move forward quickly to put the ball away.

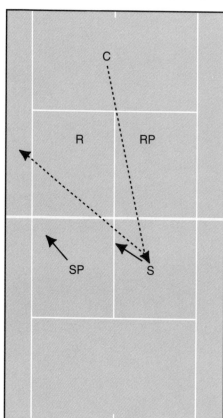

Receiving Team

As the receiver knows the intention of the server, he is instructed to hold his position until the server makes contact with the ball.

The receiver can do whatever he wants, knowing that if he lobs it can be dangerous, but if he angles back, the ball can be intercepted and put away by the server moving in.

Coach

The coach provides feedback on players' shot selection and tactics as the points unfold.

PART III
RECEIVING TEAM

Part III presents the movement and shot selection patterns that must be mastered by the receiver (chapter 6), by the receiver's partner (chapter 7), and by both players as a team once the point has commenced (chapter 8).

Breaking serve in doubles can be difficult, since serves can come quite fast, the net player is often very aggressive, and special tactics like the I formation further complicate the decision of where to return the ball. Receiving teams have to negotiate and overcome these complications. Two strategies have helped address the difficulties. The first is developing more offensive returns that avoid or challenge the net player. The second tactic is having the receiver's partner move forward more aggressively to intercept the server's first volley or first groundstroke if the server stays back. This strategy has in turn encouraged substantially more poaching by the receiving team during a match than had previously been the case.

Receiving teams have also developed six different positions or movements (see chapter 8) to use during the return. They therefore have tactical options that put more pressure on the serving team, defend better against certain teams, change the rhythm of the match, or simply form part of their game styles.

Note: All of the drills are presented only on one side (deuce or ad side). Since the receivers want to specialize on one side, consider when you set up the drills where the deuce side receiver and the ad side receiver will practice their roles of receiver and receiver's partner.

RECEIVER PATTERNS AND DRILLS

The receiver in doubles tries to neutralize the serving team on the first serve and to take the initiative on the second serve. In order to achieve this task, the receiver has five options when playing the return on his forehand or on his backhand. Two of the options are power returns and three are precision returns.

Power returns to challenge the timing of the serving team:

1. Drive crosscourt
2. Drive down the line

Precision returns to challenge the mobility of the serving team:

3. Place angle crosscourt
4. Place down-the-line in the alley
5. Lob

The receiver must identify his best two shots on the forehand and his best two shots on the backhand from these five options. This procedure follows the rule of using one's strengths to compete at one's best. Therefore, patterns

32 and 33 will cover how a player finds the best positioning on the court and how he selects his best returns according to his game style.

Regardless of a player's preferred shots, he must adapt at times against specific tactics. Pattern 34 discusses why it is better to hit more down-the-line returns when the serving team chooses formations like the Australian and the I formation.

Once he has hit the return, the receiver has the choice to stay at the baseline or to move toward the net. Pattern 35 explains how the recovery at the baseline is completely different from that in singles, and pattern 36 discusses coming to the net after the return.

Finally, a receiver does not always make the point through outright winners on the return. He needs to be ready for a second shot after the return, either at the baseline (pattern 37) or when coming to the net (pattern 38).

▌ Todd Woodbridge, one of the best doubles players of all time, handles this powerful serve with a precision backhand slice.

Receiver's position on second serve

In this situation, the receiver faces a second serve and has an opportunity to take control of the point.

Objective

The receiver needs to position himself in a way to increase the chance to set up his strong shots according to her game style. Players adopt different starting positions to receive the serve, a fact that becomes even more obvious when viewing different players return the second serve. However, since a normal position for the returning is around the baseline for the first serve and slightly inside the baseline for the second serve, we observe that differences among some players typically reflect their individual game styles.

Hard hitter (especially one with a big forehand)

Positions himself more to the backhand on second serves, to run around his backhands and hit with his forehands; this challenges the server to risk a better second serve, which could create double faults.

Quick mover or net rusher

Positions himself inside the baseline on second serves in order to take the ball early and move to the net.

Precision player

Adopts a normal position or one a little farther inside to take the second serve early and hit an angled return, with a few disguised lobs or accurate down-the-lines.

Note: the difference between the down-the-line of a power player is that she can hit right at the net player to challenge his reflexes and the precision player will try to beat him by placing the ball away from him in the alley.

All-around player

Can choose all the above options according to the conditions—surfaces, quality of serves, and so forth.

Singles retriever or counterpuncher

Often returns as he does in singles. He often remains behind the baseline even on the second serve to be able to hit a heavy topspin shot. A player that returns in this way often has his partner on the baseline to start the point. Such players have more success on clay courts, where returning serve is more conducive to using this approach.

Note: A receiver can take the new position for returning the second serve as the server tosses the ball, to disguise the intention, or he can take it right away to challenge the server to do a better second serve.

32-1 RETURN OF SERVE, POSITIONING OPTIONS

Structure

Normal points are played with only a second serve.

Server

The server can either serve and volley or serve and stay back, depending on what the receiver prefers.

Receiver

The coach requests the receiver to experience different returning positions or to experience the position which should match her game style.

Note: Have the players practice on the side they usually return from.
The figure illustrates the second serve positions normally taken by various kinds of players:

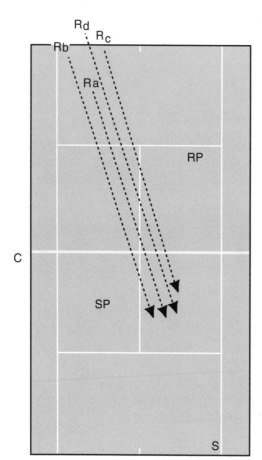

a—quick mover with chip-and-charge or drive-and-charge plays

b—precision player, taking the ball early to play an angled return

c—hard hitter with big forehand, positioned toward the backhand side to use the big forehand

d—singles retriever, playing farther back to execute a shot with heavy topspin

An all-around player can choose from among the first three options.

Coach

Gives each player feedback to help her discover the second serve returning position that best fits her game style. The coach also helps her to further understand her best second shot after the return (see patterns 6 and 7).

Receiver's five options on the return

Objective

The primary objective of the receiver is obviously to return the ball back into play. Beyond the return, he seeks to challenge the serving team, to give himself and his partner the best opportunity to win the point. When he is not defending by blocking the ball back (using a dink or lob), the receiver has five options to choose from (for both forehand and backhand) in returning first or second serves:

1. Drive crosscourt
2. Drive down the line
3. Precise down-the-line shot in the alley
4. Precise crosscourt angled shot
5. Lob

At the international level we talk about power returns. The power returns are a drive crosscourt, a drive down the line, and a drive-and-charge to the net. These returns are hit hard to give the opposing net player less time to move or to feel comfortable about poaching (he is primarily concerned with being ready if the return is driven directly at him). Using this method of returning well means that the receiver must hit about 20 to 30 percent of his returns hard down the line, to freeze the server's partner at the net. When returning in this way, players also expect that the server will be less effective in controlling his first volley. On a second serve, we may see some drive-and-charge returns.

The precision player and the quick mover use a higher degree of precision in their returns, playing away from the server's partner with the use of angles, down-the-alleys, or lobs. They also create problems for the server's first volley by keeping the ball low or by making him think about the possibility of covering a lob over his partner. On a second serve, they can use a chip-and-charge tactic.

Note: Tactically, many players will go for power with their forehands and opt for precision with their backhand strokes.

33-1 RETURN OF SERVE—FIVE SHOT OPTIONS

Structure

Live feed return drills.

For deuce side returns, the two advantage side receivers split into S1 and S2 to alternate two first serves each from the basket.

The two deuce side receivers will each return 4 serves, to practice against each of the two servers.

Players change roles for ad side returns.

Servers

Feed first serves as previously described.

Note: Can repeat the process with second serves only.

Receivers

Experiment with the five options for returns:

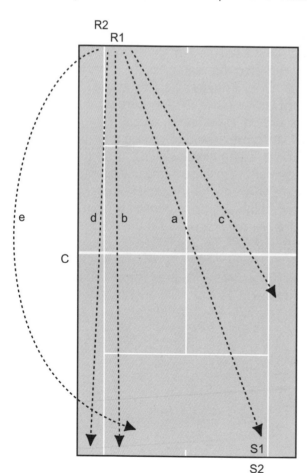

1. Drive crosscourt (line a)
2. Drive down the line (line b)
3. Precise angle (line c)
4. Precise down-the-line (line d)
5. Lob (line e)

Coach

Helps individual players discover their favored returns off a first serve on both the backhand and forehand sides.

After completing this drill, players can repeat the same process with second serve returns, maintaining their modified positions as covered in drill 32-1.

Note: Players may use different types of forehand and backhand returns to be most effective. As the second serve is easier to handle, most of the receivers will either better their return or will use the occasion to be more aggressive and choose a different shot selection.

Receiver's return down the line against the I formation

When the serving team uses the Australian formation, they are already positioned to cover a crosscourt shot, forcing a down-the-line return. When they use the I formation, however, the receiver's choices can be more confusing. The server's partner is kneeling down in the middle of the court, and the receiver may think that she can return either crosscourt or down the line. To find the best solution, the receiver should ask herself a question:

- If I don't know which side the server's partner will move to, on which side will it be less dangerous for me if she volleys my return?

To find the answer to this question, the receiver must consider her options for returning both a wide serve and a T serve. Regarding the wide serve (page 154, figure a), she reasons as follows:

- If I hit a crosscourt return, the server's partner does not even have to move (page 154, figures a and b).
- If I hit a down-the-line return, the server's partner has to move across the court, which makes the volley more difficult. Therefore, hitting down the line is preferable.

Considering her options against a T serve (page 154, figure b), the receiver discovers the following:

- If I hit crosscourt and the server's partner covers the crosscourt return, she only has to move minimally before she can easily hit an angled volley into the open court.
- If I hit a down-the-line return and the net player covers the line, once again she does not have to move a great deal but would have to volley back toward me. Therefore hitting down the line is preferable.

Objective

When the serving team is using the I formation, the best way for the receiver to counter it is by using a down-the-line return 70 percent of the time. She still needs to mix up the returns to be unpredictable.

Challenge

It is already difficult to return well in doubles without having someone who may take either side as you return. Therefore, the main challenge is to remain focused, make your decision in advance and go for your shot. Even if the net player intercepts your return, he will not necessarily win the point. As the match progresses, observe if there is a pattern in their movement for any specific serve to help your decision-making on the return. For example, will a wide serve always be associated with a poaching movement?

Execution

As a result of the uncertainty created when playing against the I formation, the receiver's partner often plays back to reinforce the defense against poaching actions.

On a wide serve (figure a), we notice that volleys 1 and 2, in reply to a down-the-line return (line a) or crosscourt return (line b), respectively, come back more or less to the same location. On the crosscourt return, however, the server's partner does not have to move to handle the ball (2), whereas for the down-the-line return, she has to move across the court (1), making the second volley more difficult.

On a T serve (figure b), the movement of the server's partner at the net is the same distance to the right or the left. If there is a crosscourt return (line b), however, the server's partner has an easy angled volley (2) to finish the point. With a down-the-line return (line a) the server's partner has a less acutely angled volley (1), and the receiver may recover in time to play out the volley.

Therefore, in response to both a wide and a T serve, the down-the-line return is preferable for the receiver and should be used about 70 percent of the time (it is still important to mix up the returns).

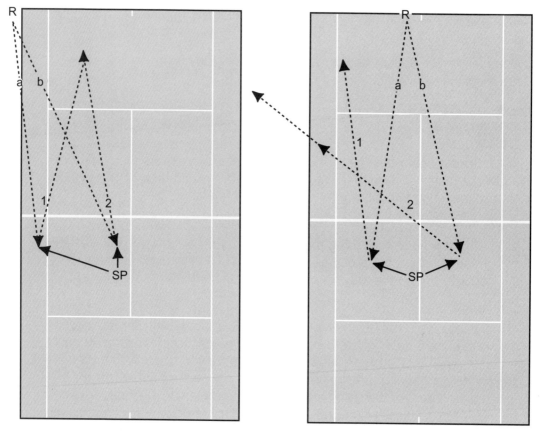

a. Wide serve return against the I formation.

b. T serve return against the I formation.

34-1 PLAYING POINTS AGAINST THE I FORMATION

Structure

Normal points are played with the serving team in the I formation on first and second serves (see pages 125-128).

Serving Team

The servers have to mix up their movements of not poaching (arrows 1) or poaching (arrows 2), although they know that the returns will be down the line (line a). This variety allows the receiver to construct her point differently, depending on whether the net player or the server volleys the return.

Receiving Team

On the first serve, implement a constraint to groove the down-the-line return (line a). The receiver always returns down the line to groove this return and to practice both being back at the baseline. On the second serve there are no constraints. The receiving team positions themselves the way they want and implements the tactics of 70 percent returns down the line and 30 percent cross-court.

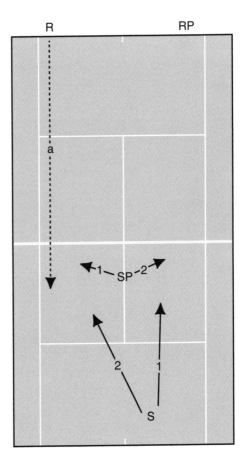

Receiver's recovery toward the alley

When the receiver stays back after the return, where should he recover to after a wide or T serve, to prepare his second shot?

Objective

To recover toward the alley on both serves, since the receiver's partner blocks the middle and forces the server's first volley or groundstroke to be aimed crosscourt.

Challenge

The main challenge is that the receiver probably also plays singles, in which players recover toward the middle. In doubles, it is the opposite recovery.

Note: On a wide serve, we sometimes stretch in singles to avoid being pulled out of court. In doubles, the receiver can move as far out as required to hit a good return. He can even choose to stay there, because the server's volley or groundstrokes will probably come back in his direction.

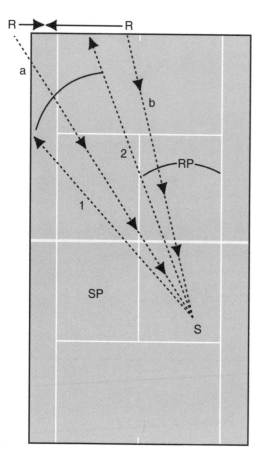

35-1 RETURN OF SERVE, RECOVERY TO ALLEY

Structure

Before playing points, the coach explains that the territory the receiver has to cover after a return is the same regardless of serve location (wide [return a] or T [return b]). The figure shows that the territory to cover is determined by the angle the server is able to create with his first volley crosscourt (1) and with a first volley that just misses the receiver's partner (2). This territory is similar if the server chooses to stay back and use his groundstrokes.

Play normal points with a focus on the recovery toward the alley for the receiver to position himself in the center of his territory, between lines 1 and 2. Better second shots should result.

Receiver's second serve return and movement to the net

Objective

The receiver must implement the tactic of coming in behind a second serve return and understand the territory to protect after this shot.

Challenge

When receiving an easier second serve even if the serve is slower, the challenge comes from the server having more time to get closer to the net for his first volley. Therefore, one of the challenges is to learn to return from inside the court and consider the possibility to chip and charge or drive and charge. The receiver has a tendency from a T serve to move in a straight line toward the middle of the court, instead of recovering to the middle of the angle of the server's first volley crosscourt options (see figure 36, page 157).

Execution

When chipping and charging, receivers should place the ball very low in an effort to attain a position closer to the net and put the serving team's volley away. Receivers should be a little further away from the net when driving and charging, but they expect that the power of the shot will create mistakes or a floating volley that is easy to attack.

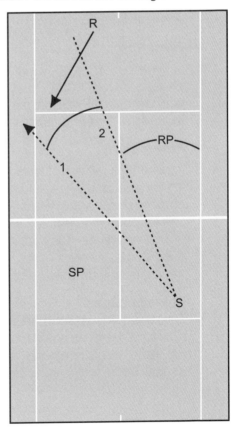

36-1 RETURN OF SECOND SERVE, COMING TO THE NET

Structure

Play normal points with only a second serve, to provide more opportunities for the receiver to use a chip-and-charge or drive-and-charge.

The coach explains the territory that the receiver has to protect after coming in behind the return, taking into consideration the territory covered by the receiver's partner. The figure illustrates that the territory the receiver must cover is determined by the angles the server is able to create with her first volley crosscourt (1) and a first volley that would just avoid the receiver's partner (2). Focus on the recovery of the receiver so that she develops better options for the second shot.

Receiver's second shot when staying back

Objective

For the receiver to discover his best second shots and to implement a planned tactic:

1. Drive down the line
2. Drive crosscourt or between the players
3. Place angled crosscourt shot
4. Place down-the-alley shot
5. Lob

Challenge

The effectiveness of the receiving team's second shot is crucial to breaking the serve. The intention of the return is to force the opponent into a mistake or to induce him to play an unconvincing first volley from which the receiving team can take advantage.

The receiver expects that his return crosscourt will be hit back to him when he stays back. For this reason, he recovers quickly towards the alley and selects his best second shots according to his game style, depending on the ball received or on his intention to exploit the serving team's weaknesses.

Execution

In general, the deuce side player hits a forehand second shot and the ad side player hits a backhand. This is one of the important considerations for choosing who will play the ad side. It is for this reason that the lefty plays on the ad side so that the receiving team has two forehands for their second shot.

Power Shots

In general, a receiver directs his drives at the weakest net player. If both players are solid at the net, however, he should hit between the two players in an effort to create some hesitation as to whose volley it is and to deny them any angles for their volleys.

Since there are many options for second shots, the receiver and his partner must discuss what to play according to their opponents' strengths and weaknesses, both individually and as a team.

Precision Shots

Typically, precision shots are played to exploit any weakness of the opponent. If an opponent has no smash, or if he is too close to the net, he must use the lob—and use it repeatedly. If he is too far away from the net, he should use angled shots, since hitting drives will not be as effective.

Drills

The receiver's second shot options have to be trained when involved in these situations:

1. Receiver returns against an opponent who serves and volleys
   - from the baseline on a deep first volley, or
   - from midcourt in reply to a short volley.
2. Receiver returns against an opponent who serves and stays back
   - from the baseline in reply to a deep crosscourt shot, or
   - from midcourt, as an approach shot in reply to a short crosscourt shot.

37-1 SECOND SHOT GROUNDSTROKE OPTIONS AFTER RETURN OF SERVE

Structure

Basket feed points.
Two players at the net simulating the serving team position after the first volley.
Two players simulating the receiving team with the receiver staying back to train his second shot groundstroke options.
Points are initiated by the coach feeding from a basket.

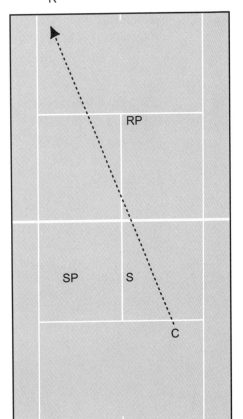

Feeds

The coach feeds easy and difficult first volleys to challenge the receiver's ability to make the appropriate decision (choice of shot) with his second shot.

Receiver

The receiver's preferred second shots may differ on the forehand and backhand sides and may change depending on the types of balls he receives.

Coach

Facilitates the discovery and improvement of players' best types of second shots according to their strengths and game styles. If you don't have a coach, identify your best two shots—if you are trying too many shots, it will be difficult to be steady.
Repeat the exercise with the coach simulating the server staying back as this will change the tactics of the receiver.

Receiver's second shot when moving to the net

Whether the receiver chips and charges or drives and charges, she needs to be ready to make a volley.

Objective

The volley as a second shot offers options similar to those used when playing a groundstroke as a second shot:

1. Power volley

When the ball is close to shoulder height, the receiver can hit the volley with good pace using a swing volley or punch volley. The best option is to hit between both opponents. Whereas some recommend playing volleys directly at opponents, it is better to aim the volleys to their side, since this tactic limits the possibility of opponents' hitting a reflex volley while protecting themselves.

2. Precision volley

Receivers are likely to receive a low ball to volley. They must stay calm and evaluate their best option:

• Down-the-line shot—used if the server's partner is still favoring the middle because the server was experiencing difficulty with an angled return.

• Angled back shot—used if the server's team is well positioned. Angling the volley back may wrong-foot the server as she recovers toward the middle and may set up your partner to take the next shot.

• Lob—used occasionally if the server's partner is still very close to the net.

Note: When the receiver comes to the net against a server who stays back, she has more time to set up and take control of the point at the net.

38-1 RETURN OF SECOND SERVE FOLLOWED TO THE NET

Structure

Cooperative playing situation from deuce side.

Server

Hits only second serves to allow the receiver to come in.
Always hits his first volley crosscourt, to train the receivers second shot.

Receiver

Returns with drop and charge or drive and charge and once at the net, chooses from the shot selection on page 160.

Server and Receiver's Partner

Do not poach; play the point out.

Note: Remember to train the receiver who plays the deuce side on the deuce side, and to train the ad side receivers on the ad side.

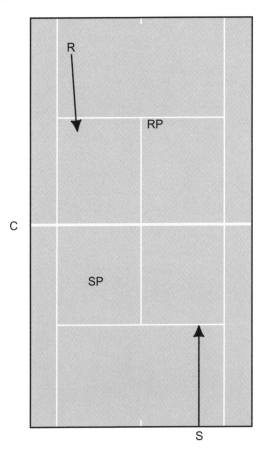

RECEIVER'S PARTNER PATTERNS AND DRILLS

7

The role of the receiver's partner is one of the most difficult in doubles tennis. It is always one of combining defense and offense, because the quality of the return and therefore, of the poaching action is unpredictable.

The receiver's partner wants to ensure the continuation of the point after the return of the first serve, while contributing to winning the point after the return of the second serve. For this reason there is a difference in positioning between the first and second serves.

On first serve returns, the receiver's partner is either at the service line (classic formation) or at the baseline (to reinforce the defense). Players are generally at the baseline when the serving team poaches a lot or uses the I formation, or when the receiver is struggling with the return and wants to play the return a little more defensively or use the occasional lob.

Since a better return of serve is anticipated on second serves, the receiver's partner (who has been positioned on the service line) now steps forward inside the service line to get ready to move forward. If the receiver's partner was at the baseline for the first serve, he at least moves a little farther into the court, to be ready to attack any short ball, or moves to the service line to be ready to put pressure on the server.

It is now common to see either

∎ the receiver's partner at the baseline for the first serve (for better defense) and at the service line for the second serve (to be ready to attack); or

∎ the receiver's partner way inside the service line on the second serve, anticipating a good return and therefore prepared to exert pressure and intercept the server's first volley.

In order to play an offensive role at midcourt with a strong presence (pattern 40) and to have the ability to poach per reaction (pattern 41) or anticipation (pattern 42), the receiver's partner also needs to assume a defensive role in his hot seat position at midcourt (pattern 39). Finally, the receiver's partner needs to know the movement patterns required when there is a lob return (pattern 43) or when the return goes back to the server staying at the baseline (pattern 44).

Modern doubles has seen a significant improvement in the capacity of the receiver's partner to instigate breaks of serve, which has resulted in countertactics like the I formation to negate the constant pressure this player can place on the server.

∎ The receiver's partner poaching per anticipation during a crosscourt rally.

The hot seat

When the receiver's partner plays at the service line, she may be attacked either by the server, volleying to close in on an easy return, or by the server's partner, redirecting a return played into her territory or poaching.

Objective

Principally, to develop the athleticism and perceptual skills required to play defensive shots effectively.

Challenge

• The receiver must say "back" when hitting a short lob or a floater, to provide her partner time to back up—thus increasing her chances of reacting most effectively to the server's or server's partner's shot.

• The receiver must let her partner know when she intends to hit the return down the line. Such notice allows the receiver's partner to prepare herself to protect the middle of the court and then redirect an eventual crosscourt volley between the members of the serving team.

Execution

The hot seat position requires the following defensive skills:

• Reflex volleys—As their name suggests, these shots are played in response to hard-hit volleys of either the server or the server's partner at the net. In this situation the receiver's partner needs to block the ball back to make the serving team hit one more shot.

• Stretch volleys—When the ball is lower, the serving team still challenges the receiver's partner by playing toward the alley, requiring a stretch volley to be played in return.

• Half volleys—Occasionally, in performing either a reflex or stretch volley, the player is actually required to play a half volley.

39-1 BASKET FEED

Because players may initially be uncomfortable in this position, fearing that they may be hit, it is better to start to train this situation with basket feeding.

Structure

Coach with basket starts the point, simulating the server's partner.
Two players rotate in the hot seat position.
Two players assume the roles of the server and the receiver to play the point out.

Feeds

The coach varies three types of feeds to the receiver's partner's volley:

1. Reflex volley—a ball driven straight at her (a)
2. Stretch volley—a ball played away from her (b)
3. Half volley—a ball that bounces in front of her (c)

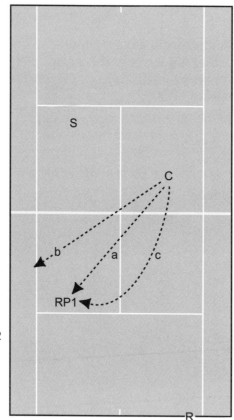

Receiver's partner's net territory

Once the serving team is well positioned at the net, it becomes quite difficult to beat them. Therefore, in advanced doubles the receiving team has learned to gamble more by having the receiver's partner move forward, forcing the server's first volley or groundstroke to be hit toward the alley or angled.

Objective

To increase the court coverage territory by moving forward and to develop the athleticism and perceptual skills required for covering the territory and reacting to volleys played from a short distance.

Challenge

The receiver's partner must learn to move in only on a good return. If not, the receiver's partner runs the risk of getting hit with an aggressive volley.

Execution

When he moves forward, the receiver's partner must exercise the following skills:

• Readiness to volley—As he moves forward, the territory of the receiver's partner expands and he has a greater chance to intercept the approach volley.

• Forcing a down-the-alley volley or groundstroke—This shot is not easy for the server since he does not play this shot in singles. Changing the direction of the shot is technically difficult. Furthermore, the server knows that if he misplaces the volley, the receiver's partner could hit the ball right back at him.

• Forcing an angled first volley or groundstroke—This shot allows the receiver to move forward and hit his second shot much closer to the net players (further challenging his reactions) or allows the receiver to approach the net right away if the server stays back.

Some teams have a rule in place to apply this pressure until they get beaten up the alley three times by each of the servers and on each side. Indeed, only one of the two servers may have the skill to redirect the volley or groundstroke effectively in the alley and may achieve such redirection only on the deuce or ad side.

40-1 LIVE FEED

Structure

One player as the server plays a first volley from a fed ball by the coach.
One player as the server's partner is ready to play the point.
Two players alternate as the receiver's partner. In this role, the receiver's partner moves in and therefore protects a larger territory.

Feeds

The coach, as the receiver, feeds difficult low returns to the server, forcing him to volley upward. This allows the receiver's partner to move forward and pressure the server.

Server

Challenges the receiver's partner only in the territory bounded by two lines of flat markers, a and b.

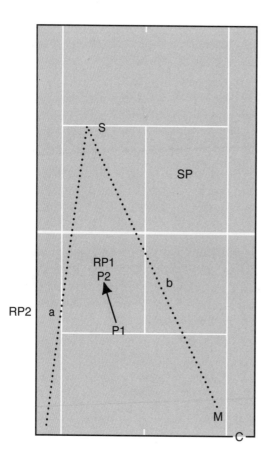

Receiver's partner

Moves from P1 to P2 to pressure the server's first volley

His territory is between line a and line b

If the receiver's partner does not touch a crosscourt volley, he looks behind to see where the ball passed in relation to the marker (M) at the baseline. If on his side of the marker, it is his shot and if outside the marker, it is the receiver's shot.

Note: the angles will change slightly depending on the position from where the server will execute his first volley. You can adjust the territory and the position accordingly.

Receiver's partner poaching per reaction

On a good return, the role of the receiver's partner is to place pressure on the first volley or on the groundstroke of the server, if choosing to stay back.

Objective

Since poaching is the ability to take balls outside of the receiver's partner's territory (i.e., outside of her immediate responsibility), the territory she covers must first be defined (see pattern 40). Once she understands her territory, the receiver's partner needs to be trained to intercept a floater when it is played slightly outside of this territory. Such interception is much easier if the receiver's partner plays closer to the net, since she will have a greater chance of playing a high volley and therefore being able to finish the point.

Note: Receiver changes sides as soon as she sees her partner poaching.

41-1 BASKET FEED

Structure

Two players rotate as the receiver's partner, who moves forward from P1 to P2.
One player assumes the role of the server's partner.
One player plays as the receiver.

Feeds

The coach feeds from the basket, starting the point by simulating a difficult low first volley for the server. The coach must also define the territory to cover (using a line of flat markers or ropes, represented by a and b in the figure) before encouraging the receiver's partner to poach per reaction (line 1). She directs basket feeds into the territory to develop players' skill and confidence, using the following progression:

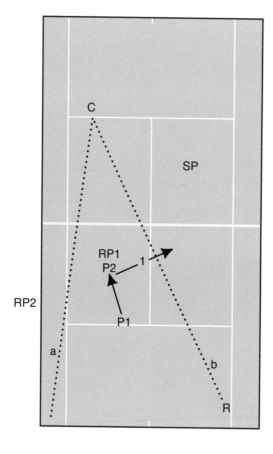

1. The coach feeds easy crosscourt shots so that the receiver's partner can practice playing the point with a poach per reaction.

2. The coach feeds some difficult angled volleys, which cannot be poached, and some easy crosscourt shots so that players can practice making decisions about whether to poach per reaction.

3. The coach feeds anything, including down-the-lines, ensuring a proper volume of easy crosscourt shots that players can poach per reaction.

Note: As they play the point out, the receiver should be ready to change sides as she sees the poach.

Receiver's partner poaching per anticipation

The pressure exerted by the receiver's partner increases if he occasionally poaches when he is sure that a first volley or groundstroke will be played crosscourt. This type of poaching is more effective if the receiver's partner has moved forward and is close enough to the net (see pattern 40) to be able to put the volley away.

Objective

To develop technical and tactical anticipation. Because it is not possible to anticipate every shot, the receiver's partner must develop an attitude of trying to anticipate the server's first volley (or groundstroke if he stays back).

Technical focus

Observe and attend to the racket angle, impact position, grip, and posture that characterize a volley hit crosscourt or down the line.

Tactical focus

Some players always volley the ball crosscourt on certain shots, like half volleys, or in certain situations such as big point plays. As soon as the receiver's partner recognizes these situations, he should be ready to change sides.

42-1 LIVE FEED

This drill is similar to the one for the poach per reaction (41-1), but the intent is different. A live feed is necessary to allow the receiver's partner to read the shot.

Structure

One player simulates the receiver and feeds balls from a basket to the coach (who is in the server's position) for him to play a volley.
One player adopts the role of the server's partner to play out the point.
Two players rotate as the receiver's partner, who moves forward from P1 to P2 to apply pressure to the serving team.

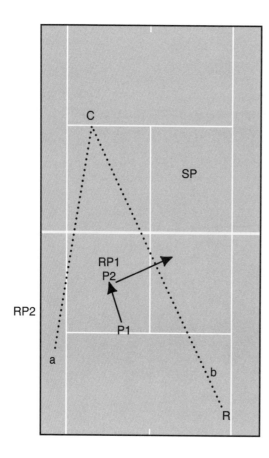

Feeds

The coach mixes up volleys crosscourt and down the line, while providing specific cues for the receiver's partner to anticipate:

- Technical anticipation: The coach asks the players to focus on seeing any differences in his body position or his impact point when volleying crosscourt or down the line.

- Tactical anticipation: The coach can also mention that he will hit all his half volleys crosscourt to trigger the poach per tactical anticipation.

Although it is a difficult drill to run, the important message this drill teaches is the attitude of trying to anticipate. As in the previous drill, the receiver should be ready to change sides when he sees the poach.

Receiver's partner's options after lob return

Lob returns are rare at the advanced level, but at the club level they are common.

Objective

To learn to take appropriate action after a lob return.

Challenge

The receiver's partner needs to react differently depending on the type of lob (offensive or defensive).

Execution

As it is difficult, even dangerous, for the receiver's partner to retrieve a smash, the receiver should let his partner know his intention to lob before the point, or if forced to hit a defensive lob return, the receiver should quickly tell his partner to back up.

After a lob return by the receiver, the receiver's partner has to be ready to do the following:

- Be ready to take up the offensive if the lob is successful and the opponents have to chase it down. Be careful not to close in too much, because there is a high probability of receiving a lob in return.

- Move back if there is time, in order to defend better against the smash if the lob is too short.

- Be ready to react if there is no time to back up.

43-1 COOPERATIVE PLAY

Structure

Normal points are played.

Server

Hits only second serves to facilitate the lob return.

Server's partner

Is positioned very close to the net to allow the deep lobs to land behind him.

Receiver

Returns down the line lobs and mixes in crosscourt drives.

Receiver's partner

Moves and plays according to the situation.

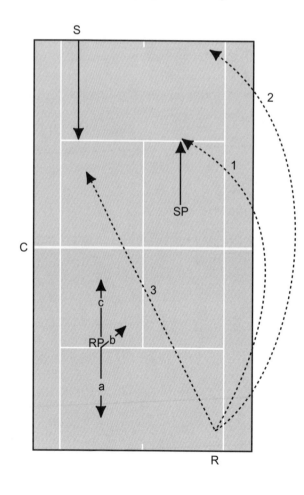

Movement

- If lob return (line 1) is smashed by the serving team:

  Receiver's partner to back up as far as he can (line a). The receiver can help by shouting "back" when realizing that his lob is too short.

- If lob return (line 2) lands behind the serving team:

  Receiver's partner assumes a net position, anticipating a lob or a weak return (line b).

- If the return is crosscourt as a variation (line 3):

  Receiver's partner moves forward (line c) to pressure the server.

Coach

The coach provides feedback on the quickness of the reaction of the receiver's partner.

Server and receiver stay back

This situation occurs when the return is crosscourt and goes back to the server, who has chosen to stay back.

Objective

Receiver's partner looks to move to the net to put pressure on the server.

Challenge

If the receiver's partner always moves close to the net after a crosscourt return, he may be susceptible to a lob or pass down the alley if the receiver's return does not pressure the server.

Execution

The figure on page 176 shows the positions for the receiver's partner on different shots:

- After a defensive or neutral crosscourt shot, the receiver's partner moves to P1—When the receiver hits a relatively easy crosscourt return, the receiver's partner moves toward the alley and only marginally forward to cover the down-the-line. He does not move too far forward, because the server should have little trouble driving the ball crosscourt and the receiver's partner will have to come back to P.

- After an offensive crosscourt shot, the receiver's partner moves to P2—The receiver's partner moves close to the net and reinforces the middle, attempting to intercept a deep crosscourt shot. This action may force the server to hit a tougher shot (such as a down-the-alley or an angled shot). The receiver's partner must be ready to backtrack to P if the server succeeds in playing a crosscourt shot back to the receiver.

44-1 COOPERATIVE POINT

Structure

Normal points are played.

One player as server hits a second serve and stays back.

One player as receiver returns crosscourt and stays back.

One player as server's partner does not poach the predetermined crosscourt return.

One player as receiver's partner positions himself according to the quality of the return and how the rally unfolds.

Receiver's Partner

The receiver's partner adopts the positions shown in the figure as follows:

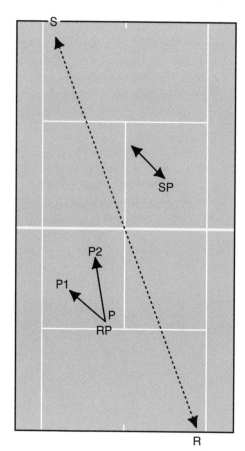

- P is a neutral position he takes until he is certain that the receiver's return or rallying shot is crosscourt and will avoid the server's partner.

- P1 is the position he takes to protect against a down-the-line when the receiver plays a short ball or an easy return.

- P2 is the position he takes to apply pressure to the server's next shot when a solid crosscourt shot is played.

Note: After moving to P1 and especially to P2, the receiver's partner needs to recover back toward P if the server succeeds in hitting back crosscourt to the receiver.

8

RECEIVING TEAM PATTERNS AND DRILLS

We have covered basic patterns for the receiver (chapter 6) and the receiver's partner (chapter 7), but the receivers also must develop teamwork. They decide together how to combine their efforts to break the serving team.

The receiving team should discuss basic tactics before the match, but they also must adjust them as the match progresses. They need to communicate in between points, as the serving team does, about how they want to play the next point. The following are some of the elements they may decide to implement:

1. Different positions or movement patterns to pressure the serving team or to improve defense

2. Different returns and second shot patterns to take control of the point

3. Poaching per command (verbal) or hand signal, especially on second serves

Team Positioning and Movement Patterns

The receiving team needs to decide on positioning before the serve is hit. The positions the receivers assume usually reflect their tactical intention on the return and their style of play. Table 8.1 shows three possible ready positions for the receiver and three for the receiver's partner.

Table 8.1	READY POSITIONS FOR THE RECEIVING TEAM	
Receiver		**Receiver's partner**
1. Classical position at baseline		1. Back at the baseline
2. Positioned a little to the backhand side to increase chances to use a forehand return		2. On the service line
3. Positioned slightly inside the baseline with the intention of taking the return early or moving to the net		3. Inside the service line, especially on second serves

■ Bob and Mike Bryan, the number one team in 2003, successfully use the both back position to defend against the first serve of strong attacking teams.

The receiving team also needs to decide their intended movements if the return is played as planned (table 8.2). The receiver has only two options—staying back or moving in. The receiver's partner has four options—staying back at the baseline to drive, staying on the service line, moving forward, or moving across to poach.

Table 8.2	**POSSIBLE RECOVERY MOVEMENTS AFTER RETURNS FOR THE RECEIVING TEAM**
Receiver	**Receiver's partner**
1. Stays back after the return	1. Stays back at the baseline
2. Moves in to the net with chip-and-charge or drive-and-charge	2. Stays on the service line
	3. Moves forward
	4. Poaches

When combining the possibilities for positioning and movement, the receiving team can show many different looks to the server and force her out of her comfort zone by inducing her to attempt different types of first volleys or groundstrokes. We recommend that receivers practice many different positions and movements so that they can adapt to any opponents, surfaces, and conditions.

Returns and Second Shots

If the receiver plans a different return to surprise the opponent, she must be sure to mention it to her partner beforehand so as not to also surprise her. Such communication is particularly important if she decides to hit a down-the-line or a lob. The receiver's partner may ask the receiver to attempt a specific return because she notices that the server's partner moves early, that the server does not split step, or some other such peculiarity of the opposing team. The receivers need to plan their tactical return patterns as a team when dealing with the I formation and with Australian or regular poaching actions from the serving team.

Many possibilities for second shots are available, depending on who will take the ball and where and on whether the ball received is easy or difficult. The second shot may be played by the receiver at the baseline, after coming in, or after changing sides because of his partner's poach. It can also be taken by the receiver's partner at the baseline, at midcourt, close to the net, or on a poach.

Too often we train the return and not the second shot, which is often the shot that actually determines the receiving team's prospects of breaking serve. The receiving team seeks to exploit any weakness. For example, if both players of the serving team are at the net, the receiving team must discuss which player it is better to drive, dink, or lob to, or which player they can simply isolate with their shots.

Poaching per Command

So far in part III we have detailed numerous patterns for both the receiver and the receiver's partner, to provide coaches and players the chance to fully develop their doubles return games. To complete this comprehensive synopsis of teamwork for the receiving team, we set forth one final pattern—the poach per command or signal—in the subsequent pages. We develop this last pattern with the three-step drill series (basket feed, live feed, and cooperative play), which offers a systematic coaching progression.

Receiving team poaching per command

Objective

The receiving team, like the serving team, can agree to poach at a specific time. Receivers most often use this poach on a return of a second serve, when the serve is directed toward the T.

The receiving team can also command a poach on every hard and low return. The main point to note is that the receiving team communicates with each other to trigger the poach.

Challenge

To execute a volley at close range while moving, facing the net, to either hit a forehand or a backhand volley (see figure on page 182).

Players must realize that no strategy guarantees the winning of a point. The poach may be unsuccessful at times; however, the bigger picture is that it creates uncertainty for the serving team and heightened anxiety for the server's volleys.

Execution

• Receiver's Partner—The receiver's partner initially moves forward as usual before crossing diagonally forward toward the net to put the volley away. Since the receiver is changing sides, the receiver's partner has to cross even if the return is of poor quality.

• Receiver—After returning, especially after a T serve where he does not have far to go, the receiver can delay the crossing movement a little so as not to give away his partner's poach. However, if the poach was commanded regardless of serve location and if the serve is wide, he should sprint toward the open court.

Drills

Since the poach per command by the receiving team is the last pattern covered, we will present the three-step drill progression—basket feed, live feed, and cooperative play.

45-1 BASKET FEED

Structure

Four players rotating as the receiver's partner.
One coach on the other side feeding first volleys.

Feeds

Coach feeds an angled volley (line a) and a crosscourt volley passing through the middle (line b) which is in the territory of the receiver's partner as the receiver is changing sides.

Receiver's partner

Starts inside the service line for his position on a second serve. Moves forward first to disguise the poach (P1), and then moves diagonally to be closer to the net for the poach (P2). He crosses facing the net to be able to hit a forehand volley (line a) or a backhand volley (line b).

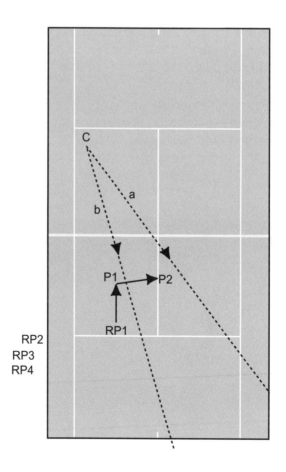

45-2 LIVE FEED

Structure

Normal points are played.
One receiver feeds a return to the coach to volley.
The coach, in the role of server, volleys crosscourt or down the line.
Two players rotating as receiver's partner to poach per command.
One server's partner ready to defend against the poach.

Feeds

Coach mixes up 3 approach volleys:

- Angled volley (line a)
- Crosscourt volley passing through the middle (line b), which is in the territory of the receiver's partner
- Down the line volley (line c) to the receiver changing sides

Receiver's partner

Starts inside the service line for his position on a second serve. Moves forward first to disguise the poach (P1), and then moves diagonally to be closer to the net for the poach (P2). He crosses facing the net to be able to hit a forehand volley (line a) or a backhand volley (line b).

Receiver

Changes sides to either cover the down the line volley (line c) or to simply carry on playing the point if his partner's poach does not conclude the point.

Server's partner

Moves back towards the service line when the feed passes crosscourt beside him.

Serving team

Competes the point to their best ability.

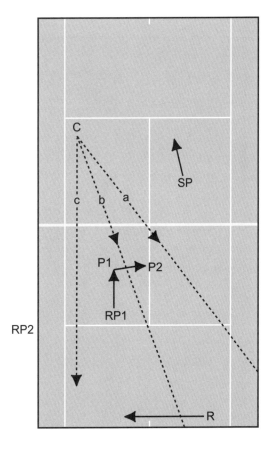

45-3 COOPERATIVE PLAY

Structure

Normal points are played with second serves only. The receiving team decides at each point whether to poach a second serve made to the T.

Server

Makes second serves only to the T, to provide the receiving team with the possibility of poaching per command off the return. The server can hit her second shot (volley or groundstroke) wherever he wants.

Receiving Team

Decides on a poach—either per command (talking) or per hand signal. They vary their intentions so as to be unpredictable to the server.

Server's Partner

Is not allowed to poach the return, since he knows that it will be crosscourt, and moves toward the center of the court.

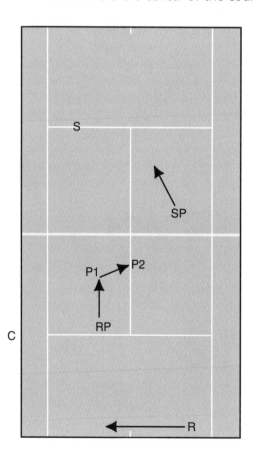

Coach

• Reminds the receiving team that, when decided, the poach per command needs to occur even if the return is not one of quality, because it may distract the server anyway and force him to change his volley at the last second, creating an unforced error.

• Encourages disguised forward movement to P1, prior to instigating the poach to P2.

• Promotes poaching that involves movement toward the net (P2) instead of only laterally.

• Asks the serving team to share the experience of having the receiving team poaching per command on their second serve.

PART IV

TACTICAL PATTERNS

Doubles patterns should be part of every training program. When players practice patterns, they not only improve their doubles game but also refine several of the technical and physical skills needed for successful singles play. In other words, doubles training benefits the serve, the return, the midcourt and net games, speed, reactiveness, coordination, and footwork—all of which are crucial for both singles and doubles play.

The challenge in planning the training sessions lies in the fact that there are so many tactics. Therefore questions quickly arise about which patterns to train first, how many to work on during a year, how long to train each pattern, and so forth.

In Chapter 9 of this section we set forth how to evaluate, plan, and train the required tactical patterns, as well as how to design an annual training plan to cover these patterns. Then in chapter 10 we provide an example of how coaches or players can benefit from charting their opponents in order to plan their tactical patterns for a doubles match.

As you may have read before, a plan does not guarantee success—but the absence of planning guarantees failure.

PATTERN SELECTION AND EVALUATION

The cooperative playing situations proposed in the drill sections throughout this book give doubles players specific tactics to practice. However, in order to improve more quickly and systematically, using a coach is always preferable. A certified coach evaluates performance, plans objectives, and uses training methods to develop players' skills more rapidly. This chapter presents three sections specially designed for the coach. It provides suggestions for planning doubles objectives, evaluating tactical patterns with a specific chart, and training tactical patterns.

Planning the Program Content

The topic of program planning can fill an entire book by itself. We provide only an example of a summarized planning format, which coaches use to present their planning content to players (see figure 9.1, page 190).

To plan which tactical topics to cover, you need to consider two elements regardless of the level of play:

1. **Most frequent patterns**—Because players will use these patterns to play many points, you must not only plan for what you want to implement as a doubles game style but also for what the opponents will try to impose on your teams.

2. **Most important patterns**—What could make the difference in winning more matches at this level, according to your vision?

Once you have selected the tactical patterns you want to train, you may want to establish a plan that can range from a few lessons to a complete annual plan. If you have an annual program, you may follow this planning breakdown to identify the content of your lessons.

Annual Plan—September to August

Most programs are designed to run from September to August, since school starts in September and summer is the biggest competitive season for the junior level.

An annual plan establishes the main goals to work on during the year. It identifies the peak competitive periods of the year, the number of which determines how many developmental periods the plan covers during the year (i.e., three peaks = three periods).

The example we are considering, National Canadian U-16 level juniors, has three periods leading to three peak competitive events:

September to December (December—I.T.F tournaments)

January to April (April—National Indoors)

May to August (August—National Outdoors)

For these three periods, the respective focal points can be as follows:

1. Starting the point more aggressively through positioning and poaching

2. Holding serve through better first volley selection against any receiving team formation

3. Increasing the chances of breaking serve through better second shots after returns

For each period, identify some specific objectives that work toward the main objective. Train these objectives over a few macrocycles (which are one-month developmental cycles).

Macrocycles

You can use several types of macrocycles (such as developmental and precompetitive), but generally a macrocycle represents a period of one month, which is long enough to provide sufficient volume and repetition to develop the desired objectives. The macrocycle is divided into microcycles, which are one-week periods designed to achieve the objectives of the macrocycle progressively.

Microcycles

Each one-week microcycle groups several lessons so that the week's training progressively achieves the desired outcome. Figure 9.1 provides an example of a plan used at a training center with a group of U-16 elite boys. It includes three 30-minute training sessions per week on doubles. This model provides a breakdown of the main objectives for the year into tactical patterns each lesson will teach. We present here only the first period of the planning (from September to December).

Note: Actual goals must identify a specific performance objective a player must reach when learning the tactics.

This type of summary planning gives the players a quick overview of what material they will cover during the year. It gives them a vision for the goals they will work toward and for how they will improve over the year.

In such a plan, you must quantify each goal by providing a concrete performance objective so that both you and the players will know exactly when they have achieved the goal. When starting any lesson, you need to break down the tactical patterns into steps to identify where a player's current abilities stand in relation to the goal to be reached.

Evaluating Tactical Patterns

Once you have planned tactical patterns for your junior program, interclub players, national junior teams, and college tennis programs, you need to evaluate them. Have your players play matches and use an evaluation sheet to gather the information you want. You can design observational charts in any way you wish. In order to give you food for thought, however, table 9.1 on page 191 provides a sample layout that is useful for analyzing three aspects of patterns of play—whether players attempt the pattern, how steady they implement it, and how effective the pattern is when successfully performed.

Annual Plan

Establish goals for the year (for the 3 periods: U-16 elite)

1. Start the point more aggressively through positioning and poaching.
2. Hold the serve through better first volley selection against different receiving team formations.
3. Increase chances of breaking serve through better second shots after returns.

Break into 3 periods

Establish goals for each period: September to December

Territory and poaching when serving and receiving

Establish goals for each period: January to April

Server's first volley selection and teamwork at net

Establish goals for each period: May to August

Receiver's second shot selection—disguise and delay

Themes for the 4 macrocycles

1. Proper positioning and awareness of the territory to protect—equally important on serve and return.
2. Poaching per reaction—maintaining territory coverage and developing the instinct to take crosscourt floaters. Introduction of poaching per anticipation, especially for serving team.
3. Poaching per command or signal when serving (more volume) and receiving.
4. Competitive period—interclub team championship. Charting and encouraging lots of movement.

Break into macrocycles

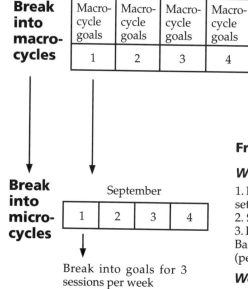

Macro-cycle goals	Macro-cycle goals	Macro-cycle goals	Macro-cycle goals
1	2	3	4

From macrocycle 1

Week 1

1. Evaluate final skill while playing points. Goal setting on position and territory.
2. Server's partner's positioning and territory.
3. Receiver's partner's positioning and territory. Basket feed for volume and for reception skill (perception, footwork).

Break into microcycles

September

1	2	3	4

Break into goals for 3 sessions per week

Week 2

1. Live feed drills for the server's partner.
2. Live feed drills for the receiver's partner.
3. Improving strokes to win more points.

Week 3

1. Cooperative points serving.
2. Cooperative points receiving.
3. Buffer period to ensure more volume.

Week 4

Competitive play (ladders, interclubs). Charting both elements learned and elements of next macrocycle.

▮ Figure 9.1 Sample annual plan for doubles training with U-16 elite boys.

Table 9.1	Example of Evaluation Chart From First Planning Period			
Patterns	**Used or not**	**Consistent**	**Effective**	**Comments**
Server's partner: poaching per reaction	YYNNYY	YNYN	YN	Needs to improve this pattern since only effective once for 6 potential poaches per reaction.
Serving team: poaching per command	YYYYYYYYYY	YYYYNNYNN	YYYNYY	Really effective when the shot succeeds. Needs quicker hands to be more consistent.

Patterns—List the patterns you want to evaluate. Identify the frequent or important patterns that players need to implement or that their opponents will use against them at their level of play.

Used or not—Indicate whether the players implement the pattern that you are looking at. For example, if a player should have attempted a poach per reaction on a ball and he did not, write N (*no*) in the column. If he did poach, write Y (*yes*). For some topics, like poaching per command, the *Used or not* column simply identifies how many poaches per command the team performed during the match, and you can compare it to the number of poaches you are looking for.

Consistent—Identify whether the skill is steady. The number of observations in the *Consistent* column will be the same as the number of Y notations in the *Used or not* column. Therefore, when a poach per reaction succeeds, write Y; if it misses, write N. In table 9.1 there are four Ys for using the poach per reaction, so there are four evaluations for consistency. Two steady poaches and two errors when poaching are noted.

Effective—When the player succeeds with the poaching volley, does she achieve her tactical objective (i.e., winning the point or keeping pressure on the opponents)? There will be as many observations in the *Effective* column as there are Ys in the *Consistent* column. Write Y in this column if the play achieves the goal and N if it does not. In table 9.1, there are 6 successful poaches per command out of 10 tries. From these 6 poaches the team won 5 points, a reasonably successful record.

Comments—Write your interpretation of your observations for each pattern. This evaluation step helps you to plan your coaching of these patterns.

You may want to chart how your players respond to some tactical situations dictated by the opponents. In table 9.2 on page 192, the coach has prepared a chart for the server. The objective is to evaluate how each player serves and volleys when dealing with different receiving team formations (positions and movements) once the point starts. The coach can use one chart per player in order to individualize feedback.

Table 9.2	Example of Evaluation Chart From Second Planning Period			
First volley against different receiving team formations	Proper tactics on first volley	Consistent	Effective	Comments
R back RP service line (normal positioning)	YYYYYY Nice deep crosscourt volley.	NYYYYY Very consistent.	YYYYY Volley penetrates, good positioning.	Has a solid deep crosscourt volley, making the second shot difficult for the receiver. Wins points on his serve very easily.
R moves forward RP stays at service line (receiver aggressive)	YYYYYY Clear intention to volley short crosscourt at receiver's feet.	NNNYY Not used to hitting angled volleys and missed 4 out of 6.	YY When he succeeded, he won the point both times.	Chooses to angle the volley, but gets nervous and tries too hard. Misses 4 out of 6, but is effective when he makes it. Needs more touch.
R back RP forward (receiver's partner aggressive)	NNYYYYYY Intercepted at the beginning when volleying deep crosscourt. Adjust tactics with first volleys (angles and down-the-alleys).	YNNYYY Misses the angle volley and is steady when volleying down-the-alley.	NNNN Lost all the points because he misses the angle and is easy to read when going down the line.	Needs to improve against this formation since he will frequently play a receiver's partner who puts pressure on the first volley. Needs to prepare with hand in front to disguise when redirecting the volley into the alley or when taking pace off to hit an angled volley. Needs also to improve decision making on whether to go down the line or angle.

First volley against different receiving team formations	Proper tactics on first volley	Consistent	Effective	Comments
R back RP poach (receiver's partner creating pressure)	N/A (never happened)	N/A	N/A	We need to use specific game situations to evaluate server play against these receiving formations since they will happen in tournaments. Also, it would be nice for players to know these variations when returning.
R back RP back (all defense)	N/A	N/A	N/A	
R forward RP forward (all offense)	N/A	N/A	N/A	

R = receiver; RP = receiver's partner

If this chart represents tendencies of the other servers as well, the coach realizes that the four players are always playing against only three out of the six possibilities offered to the receiving team. Thus, the coach asks the players to employ the other three possibilities when returning. He reminds them that future opponents may use such formations and that they themselves may eventually need to use these receiving variations. The coach also asks receivers to mix up these patterns because he wants to observe how the server reacts when these situations happen randomly. Such an example shows that regardless of the way a coach does it, evaluation is an important prelude to initiating the coaching of tactical patterns.

Training Tactical Patterns

Two methods of training tactical patterns are common:

1. Select, evaluate, and train the tactical patterns.
2. Discover tactical solutions through specific games.

Selecting, Evaluating, and Training Tactical Patterns

Select tactical patterns based on the most frequent and important ones used at the players' specific level of play, while also considering the length of time you have to work with the players.

Once you select the patterns, evaluate them in game situations. From this evaluation, you can observe three possibilities that will affect your coaching:

1. Players have mastered the pattern.
2. Players have almost mastered it.
3. Players have not mastered it at all.

Table 9.3 shows how each degree of player mastery requires a different intervention from the coach.

Table 9.3	Degrees of Pattern Mastery and Coaching Interventions
Degree of mastery	**Coaching intervention**
Players master the pattern right away.	Keep grooving the pattern through a specific playing situation. Increase the difficulty of the drill (if relevant) to reach a higher level of play by executing or receiving a more difficult shot.
Players have almost mastered it.	Provide some feedback to increase players' awareness of what they should do. Put forward some corrections of their decision making or technique if appropriate.
Players have not mastered it at all.	The pattern may be inappropriate or too difficult for them; therefore, the coach can decide to let it go. If she needs to teach the tactical pattern, the coach will proceed to a systematic 3-step progression (basket feed drills, live feed drills, and cooperative play)

Evaluating each pattern in a real game situation before teaching the pattern is important for several reasons:

• You will always have talented players who can immediately implement patterns while playing in matches; they just need to be aware of doing it. In such cases there is no need to do any systematic teaching.

• Other players are less skillful or resist change until they feel confident enough to implement the pattern in a real match situation. You must be ready to provide a systematic progression if required, through basket feed, live feed, and cooperative play (as shown throughout this manual).

An important element to consider when referring to tactical training is decision making. When players do not perform the right tactical pattern for a particular situation after you have explained it, make them focus on this specific decision by using command words to trigger the desired response. For example (at the intermediate level), when players do not decide properly when moving to the net after doing a lob that lands behind their opponents, you can execute a decision-making drill on this topic:

- If the lob lands behind the opposing team, players say "go" because they will go to the net.
- If the lob is going to be a smash, players say "back" to reinforce the defense.

Decision making can be done either before the point is played or during the point. Players must develop the ability to make proper decisions during the point. You can use four elements to help trigger such decision making:

1. The quality of the ball sent by yourself or your partner
2. The quality of the ball received from the opponent
3. The opponent's position and movement
4. Your team's position and movement

Finally, consider that technical training should follow tactical training, because a stroke becomes very specific to the situations you train. For example, you can teach the volley only when you know if the playing situation requires the reception of a fast, slow, high, or low ball, etc…and if the volley needs to be hit with pace or touch, deep or short, etc…as it will modify the technique of the volley.

Discovering Tactical Possibilities Through Game Situations

Often you can finish your sessions with fun games or playing situations that develop skills transferable to effective doubles play. Games can be particularly effective with younger players or with other groups as you deem appropriate. They can also lead players to become more motivated to learn specific skills you introduce in this manner.

Drills Using Constraints

1. No bounces allowed. Play a normal set of tennis, but neither team may let the ball bounce after the return. This drill develops the many skills needed for coming forward to the net.

2. No lobs allowed. Play a normal set of tennis, but the teams may not play lobs. Players will typically play low or straight groundstrokes or volleys. They will likely soon discover that closing in wins points more quickly, assuming that they have the skills to get that close.

3. Only crosscourt returns. Play a normal set of doubles, but the receiver can play only crosscourt returns. This constraint helps players to practice different patterns such as serve and crosscourt volley or poaching by the server's partner.

Drills Using Scoring

You can motivate players to perform a particular move more often by giving them more points when they use that specific shot or tactic.

1. Bonus points. Game of 10 points—The serving team is at the net. The returning team gets 3 points every time they drive a winner through the middle and 2 points whenever they win a point with a lob. This drill has several benefits. For example, it gets the serving team to the net to reinforce the middle and trains the receiving team to utilize a wide variety of shots, instead of just driving winners toward the alleys.

2. Super bonus points. You can decide that a team wins the game as soon as they win a point with a poach of any kind when serving or receiving.

This chapter focuses on how to select tactical patterns from an annual plan and prepare a series of lessons, evaluate a pattern before teaching it, and train patterns in creative ways. The next chapter will focus on charting the opponents and planning specific tactical patterns for a match.

10

MATCH PREPARATION

When competing, you have an overall game style that you need to respect. The possibility always exists, however, of adapting your game and planning specific patterns based on your opponent's strengths and weaknesses. Being able to anticipate and predict what your opponent will do is a great advantage to have over the other team. In this chapter you will see how you can use charting information to develop your anticipation skills, which in turn will help you to adapt your position, movement, and shot selection patterns as the serving team.

This chapter presents a three-step process of planning tactics against specific opponents:

1. Observe your opponents and scout or chart them if you can.
2. Predict or anticipate what their tactical tendencies are (from your observations).
3. Plan specific patterns to counter their strengths or exploit their weaknesses.

To illustrate this process, we choose the return of serve, since it is crucial to holding serve in doubles. Information on the opponent's returns can help determine whether you win or lose the service game.

If you can, chart or scout your opponents before the match—it helps you to plan specific tactics to start the match strongly. If not, develop similar thought processes so that, as the match progresses, you become aware of your opponents' tactical patterns and can adjust your own tactics as necessary. At the very least, take the time to do so after the match. In this way you will learn from your experience and adjust your tactics the next time you play the same team.

We hope that through this example we foster in you a desire to analyze all aspects of your opponents' games (serving, volleying, passing, etc.) so that you can put in place the most appropriate tactical patterns and therefore increase your chances of winning the match.

Charting Your Opponents

Charting is a frequent activity for a coach who wants to have precise statistics on the match. The coach uses all types of charting sheets, depending on what he wants to focus on. The sheet that follows is a possible form for charting the return of serve. The coach can chart his own players or he can chart other teams when he wants to scout future opponents.

Players do not usually have the habit of charting. If they observe their opponents, however, they can use a similar form to quickly answer at least one question: Which tactical patterns, out of the five options, do the players on deuce side and on ad side never perform (on the forehand and on the

❚ Mark Knowles and Daniel Nestor, the number one team in 2002, discuss tactics between each point.

CHARTING: RECEIVERS' SHOT SELECTION PATTERNS

SERVER: _____   **PARTNER:** _____

Opponents: (Deuce: _____ **)   (Ad:** _____ **)**

Note: Each server fills in this sheet, as the receiver may return differently according to the server and the net player.

RETURNS PATTERNS

When the serve is aimed to The return is:	DEUCE SIDE FORE-HAND	DEUCE SIDE BACK-HAND	AD SIDE FORE-HAND	AD SIDE BACK-HAND
• crosscourt hard				
• crosscourt angle				
• down-the-line; hard at net player				
• down-the-line; alley				
• lob				

(1 = always; 2 = never; 3 = sometimes)

SCORE: 1st set: _____   **2nd set:** _____   **3rd set:** _____

Note: Use one sheet per set to observe any change in the patterns during the match.

backhand)? You can answer this question before the match if you know the opponents; otherwise, you can figure it out as the match progresses or at least talk about it after the match. You will learn in the next section how this information can help you develop your anticipation skills and plan specific tactics.

When you chart the returns of advanced players (see page 199 for sample chart), you will notice that no receiver ever does all the different returns on the forehand and on the backhand. The reason is that advanced players groove their games around their strengths and practice the returns that are most likely to help them to break the server. Therefore they practice their best shots and select one or two effective variations to keep the serving team uncertain. It is common, for example, to see someone with a slice backhand hitting angled shots and lobs and using his forehand to drive hard cross-court or down the line. This ploy may give the impression of mixing up four shots on the returns, when in fact the player is using only two shots on the forehand and two on the backhand. If you observe a receiver trying all five options on a regular basis on each stroke, you often notice that this player is what we call a *shotmaker*—someone who likes to try great shots but who is often a quite erratic player.

Even if you identify only one shot per stroke that players never do, such information can be very useful. For example, some receivers never lob a return of serve with their forehands. Noticing this habit may allow the server's partner to intercept more returns effectively by playing close to the net, or it may stop the receiver from hitting his favorite shot and force him to hit a lob return that he normally never uses.

We suggest that you experiment, when watching doubles matches, with discovering which tactical option each receiver never attempts, on the forehand and backhand, and with identifying quickly any tendencies on the return of first and second serves. This observational practice develops your anticipation skills and proves very helpful when competing.

If you use a charting sheet, you may consider the following methods:

- Use a sheet for each server, since the receiver may return differently for each.

- Use a sheet for first and second serves. For example, some players occasionally lob a first serve but never lob a second serve. If you do a sheet for second serves, you may add some options like chip and charge.

- Observe specific situations. For example, are the tactical intentions on the backhand returns different against a flat serve or a kick serve?

- Use one sheet per set to observe any change in the patterns during the match.

- Use a charting sheet to observe how the receiver's partner positions himself, moves, or poaches. Note how the team plays when they are both back at baseline.

- Adapt your charting exactly to your needs, but develop the habit of scouting and charting in order to anticipate what your opponents are likely to do or not do and planning specific patterns if necessary.

Anticipation

Many players anticipate well and many do not. Those who think they do not anticipate well often believe that it is an advanced skill used mostly by the professionals. They may have thought at one point that anticipation meant guessing right, and after guessing wrong a few times, stopped doing it.

We believe that everyone can anticipate and enjoy this part of the game, whereby you can predict what your opponent will or will not do. We start by defining anticipation, in order to give you a clear idea of this concept, and then we introduce simple questions to develop basic anticipation skills.

Difficulty with anticipation comes from a limited understanding of what anticipation is. It is often defined as knowing what the opponent will do. Since it is obviously unrealistic to expect to always know what the opponent will do, and since guessing does not work, many players do not bother working to improve their anticipation skills.

We propose a broader and more realistic definition of anticipation:

Anticipation is the ability of a player to predict either tactically or technically what the opponent will do *or* will not do in specific situations.

These predictions can arise from noticing tactical patterns always or never used in specific situations. They can develop from spotting the use of technical cues that always or never lead to playing a specific shot.

To be more explicit, we will outline and use examples of two types of anticipation—total and partial.

Total Anticipation

Total anticipation means predicting what the opponent *will do*.

- Tactical—Predict what the opponent will do in a specific situation. For example, a receiver, when pulled wide by the serve, always hits down the line. When the receiver moves back after a penetrating first volley, she always lobs. By observing her game style and stroke selection, you predict that your opponent will carry out only one option in a certain situation.
- Technical—Detect cues related to the opponent's technique in order to predict her shot. For example, a specific player might always hit a crosscourt angle when using an open stance technique. Some players considerably change their impact points—they always hit crosscourt when hitting in front and always play down the line when the impact point is near them on the side. Technical anticipation may simply be an instinct that tells you that a player can perform only one shot when she prepares in a certain way or runs in a certain direction.

Partial Anticipation

Partial anticipation means predicting what the opponent *will not do*. This variety is the most unfamiliar or underrated aspect of anticipation. It is based on eliminating options. By getting rid of one, two, or even three options, your brain has less information to process. Therefore, you can react more quickly and assume an advantageous court position. For example, if you know that a particular receiver, when receiving a low volley, will never lob and never drive his second shot, you can quickly move in and try to put away an accurate angled shot or a down-the-alley.

- Tactical—Some teams never poach when serving or returning; some players never serve and volley the second serve. Sometimes it is obvious that a player cannot hit hard or cannot perform certain options because of the situation.
- Technical—You may find that a receiver playing ad side, with an extreme one-handed western backhand grip, never makes angled or lob returns when stretched wide. A server who only slices his serve never serves wide on the ad side. Finally, some players are simply technically unable to perform certain shots.

Developing Anticipation

Starting with tactical anticipation (total or partial), is easier, because it is simpler to observe only five types of returns and to notice if players always or never enact a particular play. Technical anticipation requires more experience, in order to analyze all the technical ways of hitting the ball and to anticipate what can or cannot be done.

Therefore to develop your anticipation skills, when charting or simply scouting your opponents, ask yourself these two simple questions:

1. Does the player always return the same way in this situation (e.g., a wide serve, a kick serve)?
2. Does the player never attempt a certain shot in this situation?

You may occasionally find some *always* answers, but you assuredly will find some *never* answers for the majority of players. Answering these simple questions produces several advantages.

By answering the *always* question,

- you can anticipate the intention of the player and take advantage of it, and
- you may force the opponent to try different shots, taking her out of her comfort zone.

By answering the *never* question,

- you can adapt your positioning and movement (e.g., if your opponent does not lob on the forehand, you can play closer to the net as the server's partner), and
- you can eliminate what the player does not do—consequently, you can react faster to only two shot possibilities than you could to five.

Note: Do not be fooled by a receiver who lobs and angles on the backhand return and who drives crosscourt and down the line on her forehand. She is not using four different shots but the same two shots from the forehand and backhand.

With sufficient repetition, this questioning process becomes an automatic thought process that enables you to conduct the analysis during matches. If you use this sheet before the match, discuss with your partner the tactics that will best match your strengths against the opponent's weaknesses, or any other relevant tactics. If you complete the sheet postmatch, ask yourselves what you would do differently next time.

Planning Specific Tactical Patterns—Serving Team Tactics

By making notes of your answers to *always* or *never* questions, you are likely gaining information about an opponent's specific tactics. For example, your opponent may return a kick serve to the backhand either always or never with a crosscourt drive. Observing this characteristic can help you plan specific tactical patterns. Three situations illustrate how such anticipation works:

1. Anticipating an *always* type of return (total anticipation). A particular return can happen on a specific type of serve like a very wide serve, a kick serve, or a jam serve, in response to which the receiver chooses or can only execute one type of return.

2. Anticipating a *never* type of return (partial anticipation). Players frequently do not try all the options available. You need to identify the ones that they never attempt. Often you can eliminate enough options that you have only two possibilities to anticipate from.

3. Anticipating two possibilities per stroke. This sort of anticipation—partial—is the most common type. You can often force players to try a third, different option by planning tactics that block or eliminate their preferred shots.

Tactics Against Always

The main objective of anticipating on the basis of what a player always does is to plan patterns that take advantage of this information. You can plan tactics that force your opponents to execute shots that they do not like, to get them out of their comfort zones. Table 10.1 shows examples of tactics the serving team can plan in response to particular habits of opponents.

Table 10.1   Serving Team Responses to Characteristic Plays of Receivers

Receiver play	Possible serving team responses
Always hits hard crosscourt	**Server** • mixes up the serve to deny receiver a groove on return, and • uses his partner at the net to intercept. **Server's partner** • reinforces the middle, • fakes some crossings to bother the receiver and force him to do more with the return or to change a decision at the last second so that he hits down the line, • poaches per anticipation or command while facing the net to do forehand or backhand volleys, or • implements the Australian or I formation to force another type of return.
Always hits an angle	**Serving team** • poaches per command to take away the angle return, or • uses Australian or I formation to force another type of return. **Server** • moves in quickly to try to volley before the ball gets too low. **Server's partner** • poaches per anticipation, requiring a quick run across the court to cover the angled shot.
Always hits a lob	**Serving team** • commands a poach for the server to cross and smash, especially on ad side. **Server's partner** • positions farther from the net or does not move in at the sound of the serve.
Always hits a down-the-line drive or precision down-the-alley shot	**Server's partner** • reinforces the down-the-line position as the serve is hit, and • has clear intention about where he will volley.

Tactics Against Never

The main objective of anticipating on the basis of what a player never does is to eliminate tactical possibilities. Having only a few possibilities to react to helps you to react more quickly, and you may change your court positioning. You can also design tactics that force opponents to hit shots that they usually never try. Table 10.2 lists possible serving team responses to plays or moves the receiver never uses.

Table 10.2 Serving Team Responses to Characteristic Omissions of Receivers	
Receiver omission	**Possible serving team responses**
Never hits hard crosscourt	**Serving team** • takes regular opportunities to poach per command, since the returns are not powerful drives—a strategy that leads to better volleys when the server's partner succeeds with her poach. **Server** • moves in faster to cover the angle, knowing that if the receiver does not hit hard, she will place it crosscourt. **Server's partner** • can more easily poach since she is not intimidated by the pace of the return, and • will probably be receiving lobs or down-the-lines.
Never hits an angle	This characteristic signifies that the return is most often deep crosscourt and that the player is not really a precision player. **Server's partner** • reinforces the middle to force the receiver to return an angle (a shot she has not mastered) or to hit down the line to the net player. **Serving team** • uses the I formation to force accurate placement, or • poaches per command regularly, since they do not have to move far to intercept.
Never hits a lob	**Server's partner** • moves closer to the net. **Server** • moves in quickly, since the team does not need to worry about covering a lob.

(continued)

Table 10.2 *(continued)*	
Receiver omission	**Possible serving team responses**
Never hits a down-the-line drive or a down-the-alley shot	**Server's partner** • reinforces the middle and poaches per anticipation, and • fakes poaching to induce receivers to hit down the line, a tactic that works well if there are many poaches. Many poach per command to remove the crosscourt returns and force them to hit down-the-line shots. May do also the I or Australian formation to force the receiver to return down-the-line.
Never hits three tactical options, or hits a third option very seldom and mostly when forced to do it	**Serving team** See the following section, which covers what to do when receiver is limited to two options only.

Tactics Against Two Options

Out of five possible returns, each stroke often exhibits two frequent types of shots. From these two options, it is possible either to anticipate technically which shot a player will use (according to his technique) or to anticipate tactically which shot he will use (according to the situation—type of serve, score, receiver's position, etc.). Even if you cannot anticipate which of the two types of shots he will use, you will at least be able to react more quickly when dealing with two possibilities instead of five. Table 10.3 shows possible serving team responses to possible shots by the receiver.

Table 10.3 Serving Team Responses to Receiver Shot Options	
Receiver options	**Possible serving team responses**
Backhand slice—angle or lob	**Serving team** • poaches per command since the net player can more easily handle the angled return, whereas the server can more easily handle the lob; or • uses pattern in which server moves in quickly and partner covers the lob.

Receiver options	Possible serving team responses
Only powerful forehand drives crosscourt or down the line	**Serving team** • uses I formation to confuse the receiver and force him to be more accurate by trying angles or down-the-alley shots. **Server's partner** • dominates the middle to force the opponent to play more accurately.
Two-handed backhand drive crosscourt or angled shot	**Serving team** • poaches on the type of return that they prefer if they can identify against which serve the receiver drives or angles; or • uses the Australian or I formation to force the receiver to play down the line, which is a shot he normally does not perform.
Other combinations	Serving team plans tactics to either prepare for these shots or force opponents to try other shots that they have not mastered.

Strategy is geared toward winning matches, and knowledge of your opponents can be of great value. Enjoy charting, scouting different teams, and discovering their tactical patterns. The more your opponents become predictable, the less anxious you will be going into a match and the better prepared you will be to implement your tactics.

This book regroups information on initiating the point successfully through positioning, movement, and shot selection patterns. Throughout the different chapters, coaches and players will find the information to train the most common and important patterns required for advanced doubles play. These patterns have been implemented successfully at different levels of play, from interclub intermediate leagues to the number one team in the world.

We hope that coaches and players choose to include more doubles drills in their training sessions as a means to developing new tennis skills. It is easier to learn to serve and volley in doubles before doing it in singles, and the same principle applies to the overall net game.

Remember to get the *Doubles Tennis Tactics* video (Human Kinetics) to see some of the best players in the world demonstrating the material presented in this book during Davis Cup and Federation Cup matches.

Now find the best partner available and enjoy playing doubles!

ABOUT THE
AUTHOR

Louis Cayer is known within the tennis community as one of the best doubles coaches in the world. He is the head national coach of Tennis Canada, former Canadian Davis Cup captain, a member of the International Tennis Federation (ITF) coaching committee, and the Canadian Olympic coach for the 2000 gold medal–winning men's doubles team.

Cayer has presented his workshop on tennis doubles at ITF conferences on five continents in front of tennis federation leaders from more than 100 countries. He is responsible for the Tennis Canada Coaching Certification System. He has worked with some of the world's highest-ranked men's doubles players, including the 1993 number one player, Grant Connell; three of the world's top five teams in 1996; and 2000 Olympic gold medalists Sébastien Lareau and Daniel Nestor, the latter with a number one ranking in 2002.

Cayer lives in Québec, Canada. In his leisure time he enjoys outdoor activities with his fiancé, Stella, and their four dogs.

ABOUT THE ITF

The **International Tennis Federation (ITF)** is one of the largest sport federations in the world. As the worldwide leader and governing body of tennis, the ITF has 199 member nations. The ITF is committed to extending the breadth and depth of tennis to ensure that as many people as possible have the opportunity to play tennis.

See the book's instruction on live-action video!

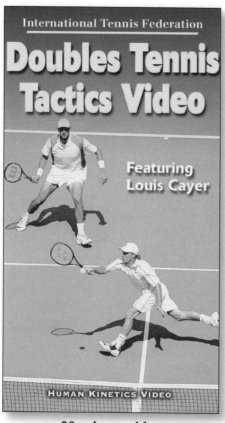

30-minute video
ISBN 0-7360-4005-6
(PAL: 0-7360-4006-4)

Developed in conjunction with the International Tennis Federation and one of the world's top doubles coaches, the *Doubles Tennis Tactics Video* presents a proven system for developing and mastering doubles play.

Featuring footage of Davis and Federation Cup play, top international pros demonstrate the patterns and drills shown in the *Doubles Tennis Tactics* book to help you practice and reinforce the correct patterns. You will learn the most effective patterns for team strategy, serving, receiving, poaching, movement, and positioning. This book-video package provides all the tools necessary to build a winning team on the court!